695

# Psycho-Ecstasy

## ALSO BY HANS HOLZER

The Prophets Speak
Life After Death: The Challenge and the Evidence
Gothic Ghosts
Yankee Ghosts
The Lively Ghosts of Ireland
Ghosts I've Met
Ghost Hunter
Ghosts of the Golden West
The Ghosts that Walk in Washington
Born Again: the Truth about Reincarnation
Window to the Past
The Truth about Witchcraft
Psychic Photography: Threshold of a New Science?
Charismatics: How To Make Things Happen by Thought Projection
The Psychic World of Bishop Pike
Psychic Investigator
ESP and You
Predictions—Fact or Fallacy?
The Zodiac Affairs
The Red Chindvit Conspiracy
Star in the East

# Hans Holzer

# Psycho-Ecstasy

## How to Awaken the Secret Powers of Your Inner Self

**Nash Publishing**
Los Angeles, California

Copyright © 1971 by Hans Holzer

All rights reserved. No part of this book
may be reproduced in any form or by any means
without permission in writing from the publisher.

Library of Congress Catalog Card Number: 70-167521
Standard Book Number: 8402-1218-6

Published simultaneously in the United States and Canada
by Nash Publishing Corporation, 9255 Sunset Boulevard,
Los Angeles, California 90069.

Printed in the United States of America

First printing

# Contents

Contents

Introduction 1

Chapter I
With Psycho-Ecstasy: Preview of Things to Come 5

Chapter II
The Nature of Man 15

Chapter III
What Exactly Are "Psychic Vibrations"? 27

Chapter IV
How to Overcome Negative Conditions and See the Results 35

Chapter V
The Second Self   47

Chapter VI
The Nature of Love   57

Chapter VII
Ecstasy: The Left-Hand Path   67

Chapter VIII
Ecstasy: The Right-Hand Path   77

Chapter IX
PSE—Psycho-Ecstasy: A New Technique   89

Chapter X
Psycho-Ecstasy and the Religious Experience   101

Chapter XI
Psycho-Ecstasy and the Creative Expression   111

Chapter XII
Psycho-Ecstasy and the Union of the Sexes   127

Chapter XIII
The Drugless Trip: How to Get High through Psycho-Ecstasy   149

Chapter XIV
Bridging the Gulf   159

# Psycho-Ecstasy

# Introduction

The more difficult the times are, the more man searches for a remedy to his ills. Throughout recorded history man has gone through various periods of stress alternating with periods of relative calm, prosperity, and peace. During the latter periods man seems to have been less preoccupied with solutions of his spiritual problems than during the time of external or internal upheaval. Perhaps periods of peace and prosperity tend to orient man towards material development rather than towards the search within. Most of the world's primary periods of illumination occurred during periods when mankind was in the throes of warfare or internal upheaval. The danger without seems to point man to search for the solution within.

## Psycho-Ecstasy

The 1970s are a period of international stress on many levels. In this country a revolution seems to take place in which age groups are pitched against age groups, economic classes against economic classes, racial groups against racial groups and, on the international scene, political extremism of one kind against political extremism of another. This is then a fertile period for man to reevaluate that which man stands for spiritually. It is no accident that more occult groups are springing up every day as time goes on and mankind more and more turns to unorthodox methods of satisfying the craving for illumination.

This book is a practical book in that it will deal with ways and means of self-realization and mind expansion applicable to everyone reading it. Moreover, the methods and techniques here given will in no way cause harm to body or mind.

Psycho-ecstasy should not be confused with, or even compared with, metaphysical methods of self-realization. There are now on the market countless books dealing with various phases of metaphysics, from outright religious practices to philosophical doctrines. They seem to have one thing in common: their vagueness and often a hint that all other methods are not nearly as good. The nature of the information in the present work is such that no special belief in their efficiency is required. I have never held that believers are particularly good subjects for psychic expansion. Belief, in my definition, is nothing more than the uncritical acceptance of something you cannot prove objectively. Naturally, hostile attitudes toward the possibility of success when using the methods given here will not enhance their success. A natural or objective attitude is always best when dealing with new and unusual methods.

## Introduction

Psycho-ecstasy is dedicated to those who search for the better life on all levels, spiritual, mental, and physical, and who have not yet found a safe and practical way to achieve it. Much of the material in this book has never been published before either by me or others. It is the result of fifteen years of intensive study, much experimentation with actual cases, and the firm conviction that it works.

## Chapter 1

# With Psycho-Ecstasy: Preview of Things to Come

Picture this, please. You've just received an invitation to a swinging party and you'd love to go. Only, what are you going to do about *it* once you get there? You know what the problem is. It's a long way from dreaming to reality. What's the point of going and feeling more frustrated than ever?

Suddenly you realize that you are no longer the same person you used to be. You have learned techniques to make things happen. How could you have forgotten?

So deeply ingrained are habit patterns that it may take you a while to remember you are no longer unable to cope with simple desires. Forget the old ways, the old hangups; you have finally found the key to open up the door to a fuller, more meaningful, and more effective *you*.

## Psycho-Ecstasy

Where's that invitation again?

Before long, you're pushing your way through a crowded, noisy, smoke-filled room. The atmosphere is loaded with the excitement of the unknown, humanity rubbing shoulders with humanity, relationships hanging in the air, promises of unfoldment yet to come.

In the old days, you would have been frightened by all this. You would have made straight for the safest corner so you could "study" the crowd. That was your way of excusing your lack of action. In the old days, you would hope someone would notice you and the miracle of contact follow. You wanted as little to do with it as possible. That is if you are the introverted type. If, on the other hand, you're an extrovert, you'd be in there in the middle of the fray, talking, shouting, glad-handing, and generally creating waves.

Only, deep inside, you were still waiting for the miracle of contact. Your extroverted attitude didn't necessarily do it. People do not like loudmouths or aggressive types. Maybe you would be better off sitting quietly in that corner. That way some member of the opposite sex might think you were something special. Which you are, of course. In your own mind, that is. How to convince *her,* and make something of it—that is another matter.

But now things are different. You have studied some new techniques and you know they work.

Quickly, you survey the room. Through the haze you see people, feel them out mentally, and wait for some sort of reaction from within you. Over there, that pretty girl. Or, if you who read this are a pretty girl yourself (or even a not so pretty girl), that interesting looking guy. Competition does not worry you. What do they know? They probably never heard of your secret weapon, those new techniques you have just learned to master.

## *Preview of Things to Come*

Something within you clicks now. There is another person across the room and you'd like a contact. It feels exciting. You find a comfortable spot where you can see the person of your choice while at the same time being reasonably free from interlopers or casual conversationalists.

Close your eyes for a moment. Visualize the desired stranger's face or appearance, as far as you can tell from the distance. Hold it firmly for about two seconds or so. Then dissolve this image within your mind into the next scene: you see the stranger look at you. You look back and the two of you "hook" eyes.

Quietly go over this suggested scene a few times in your mind. Then open your eyes quickly. Stare in the direction of your quarry. If you've done your homework well, your stranger will stare right back.

Phase Two: Keep up the contact, no matter who walks in between the two of you. Relax while you do it and don't allow extraneous thoughts to enter your mind at this moment.

As soon as you have eye-to-eye contact with the strange person, visualize the next step. With eyes open, of course, repeat within yourself the words, "Come on over and talk to me," a few times. Then quickly turn away, close your eyes again, and rest for a moment. Don't turn back to look if your object is coming over. Wait, and you will find the seed has taken root: Casually, as if it was his or her own idea, the stranger will saunter over towards you. Be prepared to receive the first blow. Don't worry about it, don't shrink from it, and don't let it die then and there. You must realize that the other person is in no way aware of being "called." Don't destroy your work by hinting that you've made them come to you. Don't play Mephistopheles. Be yourself. The stranger will smile at you or in some other way indicate that a contact is now in order. It does not really matter whether you speak first or not. The important thing is that whoever speaks also gets a reply and the conversation continues after that initial icebreaker.

Chances are the first few words are pleasant and meaningless except that they would not have been spoken had you not caused the contact by "tuning in" on the stranger.

After the initial lines, be sure and switch to some more meaningful conversation. Find offbeat interests about the new acquaintance—the dress or jewelry, if a girl; the sharp clothes, if a man—or the odd piece of art in the place or some music that is being played and needs to be commented upon. Put in a hint of your unusual talents, profession, work, outlook—enough to make the stranger curious and give her or him an excuse to query you further. That part is pure common sense and not extra sense at all.

When you have warmed up your new acquaintance to the point of discussing an evening together, your old self might again drop matters. What if she rejects me? the old personality wonders. Or, if you're a girl, what if he rebuffs my hints that I want to see him again? I'd die, wouldn't I? But then you remember with delight that you have learned some new approaches to all this. And you apply them.

Here your own approach to the social picture will determine what it is you want next. If you're a man, chances are you'll want to make it with the girl, the sooner the better. If you're a female, you'd want to "do things" with the new boy, be entertained, share some form of action, before you decide whether or not he's the type *to bed with.*

Either way, the wish can be visualized mentally very simply. The picture is formed in the mind of the "operator" now, with appropriate word command accompanying it for emphasis. Be sure and make the message crystal-clear and brief, and repeat it a few times in a low-key mood. Nervous concentration has negative effects.

Then switch your thoughts to a totally different chain of subject matter, away from the command. A few minutes later, repeat the process and then switch to something else again. If you have had a good initial eye contact and have not lost your position during the talk stage, the percentage of success here will be very high. Within a matter of minutes, the other party will suggest exactly what you had wanted her or him to do.

This is not cheating or making people do things against their will. Nobody can be made to do anything in conflict with their true inner desires. But a lot of people are not aware of those desires. They become conscious of them only when they are awakened by methods loosening the bonds between conscious and unconscious minds, such as hypnosis, or by subliminal suggestion and the techniques here described. It was all there to begin with. You just wake it up.

Let us assume your problem does not lie at the swinging party. The hangup is at work. You know you're bright and you should be way up on the ladder of success, but somehow you don't seem to move at all. You start analyzing yourself. Are you really qualified for the executive position you want instead of this clerk's job you have? You agree with yourself. Absolutely, you have the know-how, the ability, the drive, and the interest to make good upstairs where the executives work.

You talk to your boss. He nods understandingly. Of course you want to advance. So does he. He hasn't made it yet much farther than yourself and he doesn't like it much either. But he is content with matters as they are, so long as he rules the roost in his own limited sphere of influence and power. He promises you that he will bring you to the attention of the people upstairs.

He may pay lip service to his promise. After all, if you're really as much of an asset to the company as you claim to be, bringing you to the attention of the brass may enhance his reputation as a good company man. On the other hand, if there is a better job to be had, shouldn't he, who is so much your senior, have first crack at it?

You realize soon enough you won't advance "through channels" if you're in a hurry to go places in the company.

This is when you turn to the new techniques and decide to give them a try.

You acquaint yourself with the name of the man who hands out the big promotions. You make inquiries about his personal habits, his status, his home life, his accomplishments in the company, even the school he went to.

Then you study his habits, his daily schedule, and pinpoint the time and place where you are most likely to run into him alone.

Next, you prepare yourself for the big event. You put your desire into concrete form. Not, "I'd like a better job with more responsibility, Mr. Jones, because I'm good." Not, "Couldn't you give me a break, Mr. Jones? I mean, let me have a crack at something really big?" He could not care less about your wishes.

"Mr. Jones, I've got a couple of ideas on procedure that may well save you money and I'd like a chance to discuss them with you *directly*," or, "Mr. Jones, could you spare me an interview sometime? I've been with the company for____ years, and I've observed a couple of things that make me believe I could suggest a few procedures of great impact on your profit margin," or whatever applies more closely to the business or professional situation you're in.

In other words, don't think of yourself. Think how you can show him that spending his valuable time with you, minor clerk, can mean dollars and cents to him. Nothing else is any good, no matter how enthusiastic you wax about it. Be sure, however, you have some really workable ideas. Don't fake it. He does not have to buy them, but he may be impressed by you if they *ring true.* He may feel a guy who has some new ideas that cannot be used but are constructive and sensible might also come up with some more accurate and usable suggestions in the future.

When you have eventually reduced your opening gambit to one sentence, or two at the most, repeat it a few times in your mind in a relaxed mood. The night before your planned attack, visualize yourself catching your Mr. Jones off guard at the predetermined place and time. Close your eyes and see the scene unfold in your inner mind. Hear yourself say the phrase and hear him nod agreement. Then go to sleep. The next morning, just as you awaken and before you are fully awake, repeat this process once more.

Forget it until the time comes to put it into operation. Don't keep visualizing it all morning while on your job, until you're worn to a frazzle.

A few moments before you take the elevator up to the executive floor or wherever it is you are going to waylay Mr. Jones, let it flash through your mind again for the last time. Then make your mind a blank, breathe deeply, feel the idea of "success" permeate your whole being, and go to it.

Your chances of success are great indeed, if you haven't goofed along the way. The moment you lay eyes on your Mr. Jones, keep your eyes glued onto his. Hold this contact and

## Psycho-Ecstasy

send him the message. "Say yes," or words to that effect, as you unspool your preplanned attack.

You can use this technique, which I first mentioned in a book called *Charismatics,* in almost all situations. Visualization in a low, relaxed key, as if it did not really matter if it worked, followed by verbalization and a confident attitude, are the key factors. The initial eye-to-eye "hook-in" is very important, as it establishes a direct beam between you and the other person. On this beam, small particles of your thoughts—energy programmed with emotional stimuli created by you—reach the sensitive areas of the subject you want to influence, and the result is almost always positive.

The first step to full realization of man's potential lies in the extension of his natural powers. What passes for a human being these days is nothing short of a caricature of man. Large potential power reservoirs of the mind are empty because the average person does not know how to fill them. Entire facets of personality are either ignored or relegated to the realm of fantasy, delusion, and fallacy. People are told their sense of imagination is to be feared as misleading and their logical sense of reality must be stressed at all times. That is like saying to an automobile: Be sure your gears are well oiled, your steering wheel straight, your windows clean, and you'll get any place you like. You don't need a driver.

Only through the gateway of the emotional self does man learn to understand the forces of nature and himself and the powers nature has given him as his birthright. The Charismatic techniques were designed to allow people to make things happen for them by a combination of sensory and extrasensory methods. The result is a better, more satisfying life on all levels—a sense of accomplishment coupled with a sure knowledge that the power lies within man, not in a machine or greater scientific knowledge of the material world.

But these techniques assure man only the three-dimensional life in which the personality functions at desirable levels compatible with the best that nature allows man to experience. They are not designed to lift him beyond that strata where he is most comfortable because so many of his own kind are there. It is a little like the upper middle class which lives in comfort, above-average culturally and broadly educated, and is content to experience to the fullest all the blessings that come with this social-economic security.

Beyond this strata lies the sphere of ecstasy, a rarified and demanding level not as easily reached as the levels of realization readily available to practitioners of Charismatics.

Ecstasy is not for everyone, and those who feel no need to rise beyond their level need not feel lacking in any essential qualities. The call to total immersion in ecstatic conditions cannot possibly apply to more than a fraction of humanity. Even this fraction is of course large by numbers. I suggest that only those apply themselves to the study leading to Psycho-ecstasy who are truly willing to discipline themselves as required and whose needs cannot be satisfied otherwise. To get to the end (ecstasy), one must start at the beginning (man). If this sounds strange or obvious, it is neither. Common concepts of the nature of man are not necessarily correct from the point of view of the esoteric student. It is best to bring nothing more into this study course than one's good will. The rest must be learned along the way. Previous notions, no matter how well-meaning or respectable, should be left behind.

## Psycho-Ecstasy

In a way, the future *adept* is reborn into the world of Psycho-ecstasy. He does not enter it loaded down with alternate concepts.

It is futile to jump ahead and look for the final steps in this program as a shortcut to the desired results. Only by studying these pages in an orderly, progressive, step-by-step fashion, will the reader arrive at the desired result.

*"Eritis Sicut Deus"* (You shall be as God), wrote Johann Wolfgang von Goethe, as the *leitmotiv* in his *Faust*.

To be God, one must first be Man.

## Chapter II

# The Nature of Man

In order to understand what man can do, it is absolutely necessary to understand what man is. This is not as obvious as it sounds. Various people have different opinions regarding the nature of man. To the orthodox believer in religion, whether priest or layman, man is simply that which God has created in His own image somewhere back in history. He does not question the uniqueness of man's creation nor the sudden appearance of man upon the Earth by divine fiat. This attitude is common with all religions whether Eastern or Western, and it even applies to polytheistic cults. Whether a single god or a multitude of deities is responsible for the creation of man, to the religious person he is still the end result of some form of supernatural intervention. It is

## Psycho-Ecstasy

amazing how rarely a religious person questions such basic beliefs. For instance: What happened before man was created by the deity? Was there simply chaos, nothingness, a state of turmoil? And if so, why did God decide at that particular moment to fill it with the image of man? Clearly the question as to the why man was created at a given moment cannot be answered rationally at this state of science. It can, of course, be answered theologically in that one may assume God in His wisdom had decided that the moment had come to put man on earth. This puts the onus right back onto the deity, of course, and leads to still another unanswered question. Who is the deity and who was in charge prior to the existence of God and who put God in charge? None of these questions can be answered within the framework of our understanding. If God or the gods created man in their own image, as the Bible and other earlier religious sources tell us, then it follows that God or the gods are anthropomorphous—that is to say, they look like human beings.

The fallacy of this reasoning is clear as soon as one realizes that "being created in God's image" may refer to the spiritual image rather than bodily likeness. If God is a spirit and man created in His image, then man's soul is the same kind as God's entire being. What is meant by this is simply that both God and man are essentially spiritual entities, one derived from the other, but in the case of man, dwelling temporarily in a grosser envelope called the physical body. The religiously oriented person will accept such a view and the fact that man dies but somehow continues to exist in a rarely defined world of spirit. Differing from faith to faith, that world is either up there, out there at the whim of God, or simply at the end of time when a sacred bugle blows to awaken the dead sleeping peacefully in their graves. Whether one believes in a literal resurrection or simply in a vague afterlife, there is a certain expectancy of life beyond the grave in all religions. Today many people who are religious nevertheless have serious doubts as to the reality of such an afterlife and tend to consider it more of a spiritual promise than a firm reality on which one may count. At any rate, they will argue that we are not supposed to know too much about it before we get there. That, in short, is the average attitude of the religiously oriented person and it satisfies him, by and large, since under this system he is accountable to God and to himself only to the degree of his ability to do so and within the limitations of his human knowledge. People of this bent are often disturbed by scientific discoveries seemingly proving the existence of a nonphysical world beyond this one into which all of us eventually pass. They do not like to have their romanticized view of the hereafter brought "down to earth" by hard facts. The implications, such as the necessity of leading a moral life on earth, are also to be taken into consideration and there is, strange as it may seem, a tendency among many otherwise religious people to reject any notion that we can explore, by scientific means, inner reaches of the world beyond.

The religious person lives blissfully unaware of the doctrinal implications of much of formal religions. He is only dimly aware of the fact that so many laws of his church were made by men with political and ecclesiastical ambitions. In the case of Christianity, he is rarely aware of the manipulations of the Council of Nicaea, when a fourth-century assembly of bishops decided to rewrite the Bible and turn Jesus' simple emotional faith into a formalized, dogmatic, state religion. He doesn't think about the changes brought about during the medieval period when that same simple moral religion created by the man from Galilee in divine

*Psycho-Ecstasy*

inspiration becomes a complicated intellectualizing and power-structured way of life. The Son of God now has many equally sacred companions. There is, first of all, the Virgin Mary, Mother of the Son of God, and then there is a host of saints and martyrs, human beings who stood fast in times of persecution and thereby earned for themselves sainthood and a position somewhere between man and God. None of these concepts were part of the original Christian religion.

If he were a Jew, he would not think very much of how some of the Mosaic laws related to existing conditions in the Near East at the time were promulgated. He follows them blindly and faithfully even though they may be out of step with man's modern way of life. If he is a Buddhist, he doesn't stop to consider the many "small Buddhas" who have joined the original one as demigods and make religious life complicated indeed. Every religion has a tendency to add quasi superhuman personalities to the worship of the original founder person. Only the so-called Old Religion, the White Witchcraft faith of the Stone Age, never added any other deities to the original concept of the Mother Goddess and the Horned God of the Hunt.

Then there is the materialist. Whether he is the capitalistic kind or the communistic kind, the materialist rejects religious notions as so much fantasy. To him, biblical writings are simply symbolic expressions of universal beliefs and even superstitions. He considers himself a modern man who no longer needs the crutch of religion to support his existence on earth. If he has problems of seemingly emotional or mental character, he can always turn to competent psychiatric help for relief. The materialist thinks he is self-sufficient. In a way his "religion" is that of some very modern pagans who are far from being materialistic. The

## The Nature of Man

common denominator is the conviction that one is god and that everyone is their own god. While the pagan looks at himself as a god as a way of saying, "I am nature, nature is a part of me, and we are both divine," the materialist simply feels that he is god because he can control all conditions including his own state of being, and to an increasing degree, the environment in which he lives. Natural catastrophies and other events clearly indicating his inability to do so at times, he dismisses with a shrug. True, some conditions are still outside his control, but that is only temporarily so. As he learns more and more how to harness the forces of nature, he feels he will also control the environment completely. The materialist firmly believes in technology as the ultimate answer to all of his problems.

What is man in the eyes of the materialist? It would be unfair to say that to the materialist man is merely 62¢ worth of chemicals, as one sarcastic scientist said some years ago. Even the most extreme materialist does not deny the existence of the human mind any longer. Russian scientists have for years realized that the body alone does not constitute man. But both Eastern and Western materialists still think that minds can be defined as some function of personality involving a biochemical process or at least an electromagnetic process. The notion of a divine spark within man is firmly rejected by both Eastern and Western materialists. Man, of course, was not created by God in their view: Man simply evolved from the interaction of certain chemicals, primarily amino acids, in primeval times. The materialist points out that earth was originally covered with water, a fact our scientists have long established. As the planet cooled off, continents started to emerge. Simple life forms began to appear. All life, according to the materialist's point of view,

## Psycho-Ecstasy

and to a large body of scientists as well, derived from biochemical processes in the water itself. First, very simple archaic forms of life made their appearance. Eventually the ladder of evolution led to man. Hand in hand with such a view of the universe goes the Darwinian theory of man's evolution from the ape. To this day there are states in the United States of America where evolution may not be taught in schools or even publicly discussed. People no longer go to jail for it, but teachers may not include it in their curriculum. The famous "Monkey Trial," in which the brilliant lawyer Clarence Darrow defended a teacher named Scopes who had been teaching evolution some years ago, clearly proves that the idea of man's evolution via the ape is by no means acceptable to everyone in America, even today. But is man really a higher form of the ape? Is it not possible that man was a parallel creation, drawing upon physical development already reached in an earlier species, the ape, but separate and different from that species? That at least is my own view.

In the materialistic point of view there is no room for soul or spirit within man. The functions of the mind are explained simply as invisible but nevertheless tangible forms of activity created by the human brain. The materialist makes a great deal of the size and shape of the human brain and will not even discuss any scientific evidence pointing towards the existence of the nonphysical component within man, that which religion calls soul. There couldn't be such a component, in his view, since no one has ever found it or visibly demonstrated it, he argues. "I cut up a body and I find no soul," stated the late German surgeon, Dr. Sauerbruch. The materialist clings to that view. Any form of visionary experience, whether religious or psychic in nature, he explains with the blanket term of hallucination, inferring that such experiences must, of necessity, be due to illness or imbalance. Neither the materialist nor the religiously oriented person has any relationship to the principle of reincarnation. The orthodox religionist ascribes man's destiny to God's will and man's efforts. Nowadays, perhaps, he may give a passing nod to the environmental conditions, economics, and other marginal influences. The materialist, on the other hand, makes much of hereditary factors, man's chromosomes, environmental conditions, and political and social influences. There is no room in his philosophy for God's intervention or intention nor, of course, for faith. Curiously enough, while the materialist does not care to even discuss the possibility of predestination and fate, he accepts the existence of luck and chance, never stopping to analyze what exactly luck and chance are, how they operate and who has put them into motion.

Today there is a third path to understanding. It is the esoteric road which attracts increasing numbers of people who have become disillusioned with both materialistic and religious points of view. *Esoteric* here simply means "from within" and implies a way of life in which the physical and the spiritual are in balance. I have no doubt that the esoteric view represents truth, or as much truth as man will ever know. There are areas of knowledge where an explanation in terms we can understand is impossible. When we reach the rarefied atmosphere of the "masters of destiny," the deity itself, and the inner workings of spiritual law, most people find it difficult to comprehend how all this works. What we do know, however, is sufficient for practical purposes of daily living, sufficient to make our purposes clear to us and to build useful and exciting lives upon a concept that is neither mysterious nor fraught with threats, coercion, or compulsion of any kind.

## Psycho-Ecstasy

To understand what man really is, start from the end result and work your way backwards. This is in opposition to the religious and materialistic points of view which like to begin at the beginning—that is to say, the creation of man or the entrance of man into the physical world. Esoterically speaking, man is a dual being. He is first of all an electromagnetic field into which are programmed certain stimuli, impulses, ideas at the time of birth. Each and every personality differs from the next, but they are identical in *technical aspects* and in the way they function through the sensory apparatus. This energy force representing human personality is infused into a physical body at the moment of birth. As time goes on, it becomes more and more familiar with its physical vehicle and fills it to the best of its ability. As time goes on, environmental influences such as love, education, and physical factors help shape the way in which this energy field operates in the physical world. The basic structure, qualities, and nature of each and every individual personality are already in existence at the time when spiritual force and physical body are united, but the development of this basic pattern occurs during the lifetime on earth, when it may undergo changes, improvements, or deterioration. At the end of life in the physical body the electromagnetic field within it has taken on the outer characteristics of that body. Thus, when the dissolution of body and spirit occurs at the moment of physical death, the inner esoteric body is ready to take over the functions until then exercised by the grosser physical body. We know from many recorded instances of apparitions at the time of passing that the newly dead person looks no different from the recently deceased and that, in fact, the inner body is an exact duplicate of the outer body, especially at the moment of death. It is a little like the inner skin of a

## The Nature of Man

fruit which is more sensitive, finer, and therefore capable of greater variation and reaction to the world in which it exists. The esoteric body, which is what we take with us when we die, is capable of accomplishing anything we can do within our thought processes, including almost instantaneous removal from one location to another. In addition, it has all the characteristics of the former physical body, and thus feels and reacts to touch pretty much as it did when it was still the inner layer of a grosser outer covering.

All creative thought processes occur in the mind, not the brain. The brain is merely a switchboard through which the mind channels its commands and impulses. It is a little like a complicated electric maze in which the nerve fibers function similarly to electric wires in man-made contraptions. Mind formulates thoughts which are sent out to both the body and the world outside via the brain, but mind and body are not the sole components of man. There is a third force—in fact, the highest of the three. That which religion calls the soul and which in parapsychology is often referred to as psyche or psi factor is, in fact, personality itself. It is emotional in character and made of energy, as is the mind. I prefer to call it the spirit in this context since it embodies the active, creative, and original element in man. Man then is a triple combination of spirit, mind, and body, functioning in unison in a descending order. That is to say, body without mind and spirit cannot live. Mind without spirit cannot live. But, spirit by itself exists in the higher realms of consciousness. In many philosophical theories mind and spirit are either confused with each other or presented as one and the same principle. Clearly they are not, for mind is an intellectual force free from all emotional connotations, while spirit is purely emotional, free from all intellectual connotations. It is important to know what facet of one's personality should be brought into play under certain conditions to accomplish definite aims. To lift a heavy object, body and muscles must come into play. To answer a difficult question requiring logical thinking, clearly the mind must be used; but to come to an emotional conclusion or one involving religion, only spirit and the emotional inner self can hold the answer.

For something to exist in this world, it need not be visible. The air around us is hard to see with the naked eye and yet we know it exists because we have tested its existence. Mind cannot be put into bottles but its workings are clearly observable in its results. Anyone who has ever observed a religiously uplifted person during a church service knows what the spiritual excitement within can do to that person's appearance, and yet we cannot touch spirit the way we can touch a piece of wood. Gross physical actions require bodily involvement. Mental concentration produces a higher form of action such as telepathy—mind-over-matter phenomena as demonstrated by Professor Joseph Rhine. The highest form of action comes from spiritual involvement. Yet, all three elements within man—spirit, mind, and body—are of the same basic materials. Nothing in this universe is made up of nothing. All three elements in man are part of an electric force, an energy that is the basic energy of all life whether spiritual or physical. Spirit, mind, and matter differ only in the density of this force and not in the nature of it. The thicker the concentration of the energy force, the grosser it appears. When the energy force is at its densest, it becomes matter and represents the bodily functions in man. When it is of a thinner, more spread-out kind, capable of reaching further because of it, it is the stuff of which minds are made; and when it is at its finest and most sensitive, then this same

## The Nature of Man

energy manifests itself as spiritual force capable of even greater accomplishments than the other two.

The first step to self-realization is a full and complete understanding of what one is. No one can use the powers within until such time as one has fully understood what they are, by whom they were created, and what their nature is. Only by realizing that man is a triple unit and that each of the three elements can accomplish certain things as no others can, do we grasp the enormous gap between what man has accomplished and what he is still capable of accomplishing. With the exception of a few rare individuals called *adepts*, who have known this throughout the ages, the majority of mankind has made no use of these dormant tools of greater knowledge and self-improvement. Now that we are standing at the threshold of disaster in our material world, perhaps it is more timely than ever to take stock of our real inventory and bring all forces within us into play before it is too late. While man is composed of three elements—spirit, mind, and body—two of these, spirit and mind, exist and function in the so-called "ether" or the nonphysical half of our world. The other element in man, the body, rules supreme in the physical world we know. Thus, it is a dualistic world in which we live. Not only does man have an unphysical half, but so do animals and plants, anything that lives.

It is important to realize that our universe is dualistic in nature, when implementing the techniques I have worked out in this book. Only by fully understanding the interplay of the three elements in man in this dualistic universe will we make full use of the dormant power within us. The nature of man is not monolithic; but, like an iceberg, his greatest assets are below the surface of consciousness. Therein lies both the danger and the blessing.

## Chapter III
# What Exactly Are "Psychic Vibrations?"

Up to a few years ago the term *vibrations* was rarely heard outside esoteric or psychically oriented circles. It was a term reserved strictly for believers, for those dabbling in the occult, and was frequently held up to ridicule by interviewers and anyone not familiar with its connotations. Today, everyone among the young and many among the not-so-young speak of "vibes," which is short for vibrations. People say that the vibes in a certain place are good, or that on entering a certain room they receive positive vibes, and they will inquire how the vibes are before visiting another friend. Expressions like, "I get good vibes from you," or "Your vibes are getting through to me," are heard more and more frequently. The word *vibration* merely means the *measured* up and down movement, or the back and forth movement of a certain object or person. To vibrate means to be in movement without actually leaving one's position. Buildings vibrate when traffic passes by. Musical instruments vibrate when struck. The airflow into our larynx makes the vocal cords vibrate and thus produce sound. The mating call of certain insects is produced by vibrating part of their legs. Airplanes vibrate in flight due to the action of the motor. Electric massage machines derive their beneficial actions from their vibrations produced through electric motors. Vibrating means also to shake up tissue or matter for various reasons and with varying results. The wrong kind of vibration may cause an earthquake. The right kind of vibrations may cause healing in the human body. In a way, vibrations are related to the act of shaking up. When something or someone is shook up it requires the action of an outside force or of another individual. When vibrations are involved, however, no secondary source is necessary. An object or person can vibrate of its or his own volition. Thus, shaking up is from the outside in, and vibration is from the inside out.

Psychic vibrations are more like radiation or radio waves in that they are invisible but definitely perceptible. The basic difference between ordinary vibrations of one kind and another, such as I have just discussed, and psychic vibrations is the fact that the latter are not stationary but, in fact, are going out to another individual or into various directions. In this respect they resemble radio waves or cosmic radiation. Psychic vibrations may cover or fill the individual who creates them, but they are also traveling, reaching out from the center, and are never stationary or self-contained. They are essentially flows of psychically charged particles, emanating from the thought and feeling center of one person, and directed outward either towards another individual or towards broad, undefined areas. When these flows of magnetic energy reach another person's sensitive areas, a reaction results. Sometimes this is consciously registered; more often it is subtle and unconscious but always resulting in some form of action, change of attitude, or other acknowledgment. When the flows of psychic vibrations are directed and deliberately channeled, or when these actions are undertaken between consenting people, so to speak, in tune with each other, then of course the results are even more astonishing and their impact upon the personality very great.

The vibrations are the carriers of the psychic impulse. As carriers they do not have feelings or emotional connotations. They are simply energy flows. The psychic particle, riding, so to speak, upon the vibration emanating from an individual, reflects that person's emotional message. This message can be conscious or unconscious and its strength or depth will depend upon the individual's ability to project psychic energies. There are three kinds of usage to which psychic vibrations can be put. First: Psychic vibrations may be used by an individual to scan a place or person for impressions and to bring back that information to the individual's consciousness, thus informing him of something he cannot know through the ordinary five senses. For example: Alexander B. had problems accepting disappointments from those he had trusted. By nature a very generous person, he had had several business partners and, in each case, had found himself at the losing end after some time. In each case he had judged his partners wrongly and trusted them when he should have been more cautious. He did not have the ability to evaluate these people properly until he discovered the principle of psychic vibrations. When he became aware of his talent in this respect he immediately and dramatically improved his business success. On the very first occasion after this discovery, he "sent out" his psychic vibrations towards the man who wanted to go into partnership with him. Immediately he received a negative response with an intuitive warning not to trust that person. Acting upon his own intuition, he rejected the offer for partnership. Two months later he read in the press that the same man had been arrested for embezzlement. Had Alexander B. not used his psychic vibrations to scan the other person's thoughts and emotional patterns, he would have again suffered a loss.

Secondly: Psychic vibrations may be used to contact another individual or, in turn, be contacted by another individual for the purpose of personal relationships, especially where personal inhibition, shyness, and fear might prevent any overt action on the part of the one desiring that contact. By use of psychic vibration waves the contact would be established without the need for spoken language. Action and conversation would naturally result once the psychic vibration contact had made this possible. Tuning in on another person or allowing oneself to be brought in tune with someone is almost like telepathic communication except that no actual words are exchanged. Rather, it is a deep and sudden acknowledgment of contact that one accepts as natural and proper.

Thirdly: Psychic vibrations may be used to look into the future or the past of a given place, situation, or person. All professional mediums use psychic vibrations as the tools of their trade. By use of these energy waves they are able to read that which has transpired unknown to them or that which will happen in the so-called future, even though consciously they have no way of gaining this knowledge.

## Psychic Vibrations

We create psychic vibrations within our personalities through a combination of autosuggestion, command to "reach out," and thought projection. With more emotional individuals this may be partially on the unconscious level. Everyone is born with a certain amount of life energy. Part of that life force is used to send out psychic vibrations. Some part of this energy is spent and not returned, thus creating states of fatigue if psychic vibrations are allowed to be sent out too frequently without adequate rest in between periods of contact. This also accounts for the fact that most professional mediums eventually reach a plateau where their force seems to be exhausted. Sometimes they have a comeback some years later but sometimes they take it to mean the end of their professional careers as psychics. There is just so much life energy within any of us, and once it is spent it cannot be replenished. Anyone who has the ability to send forth psychic vibrations and is aware of it will notice the same ability in another person. About one in ten people have it. Those who do not manifest it may very well also have it but in such an undeveloped state that they are not aware of it. Frequently psychic vibrations are part and parcel of effervescence, charm, strong personality, and all the other things that make one person stand out over another. We often refer to a "magnetic personality" when, in fact, we become conscious of that person's psychic vibrations. This electromagnetism not only attracts but it also holds attention and implants thought images in the receiver. The particles transmitted through space, or rather through the so-called ether, are in reality tiny amounts of energy coated with images of the particular sender, with desires, thought forms, emotions or expressions emanating from the sender and directed outward to a specific receiver, as the case may be. The so-called ether

## Psycho-Ecstasy

is a term applying to the air around us. While the orthodox scientist sees only air composed of oxygen and other chemical substances, the esoterically oriented individual also notices a magnetic quality in the air surrounding us. It is in this ether that psychic manifestations take place. The invisible but very tangible component of the air showing electromagnetic properties is also the conductor along which psychic vibrations move in and out.

In electricity there are two kinds of currents, direct and alternating. It has been shown that alternating current is generally more effective, more capable of delivering the work load and of being raised to a higher voltage or potential. In a similar way, psychic vibrations are more effective as "vibrations" rather than a steady stream of energy. Just as with alternating current, the fact that the flow of energy is interrupted in rythmical patterns adds to its effectiveness, so the weaving in and out of psychic energy also increases its reach and strengthens the impact. Psychic vibrations are also attention getters, especially when they are used to reach another individual. The alternating pattern of energy flow is likely to be received with more attention than a steady, even beam would be. This is similar to the siren. A steady blast on a siren does not have the wallop of a wailing sound going up and down on the tonal scale. A steady traffic light will not arrest the speeding motorist at an intersection, where a flashing light most likely will. Why this is so no one really knows except that human nature has a tendency to become accustomed to any form of steady influence. Irregular or alternating signals seem to prevent the receivers from becoming too quickly used to them, and they thus create a stronger state of alertness than a steady flow of energy or an uninterrupted pattern might cause.

## Psychic Vibrations

When we are dealing with psychic vibrations we should also keep in mind that these are not powers of a supernatural kind of a gift of necessarily divine origin any more than man himself is part of the divine spark. Even though people have different amounts of psychic vibrations at their command, and some have more while others may have a great deal less, essentially the ability to create and project such psychic vibrations is part of human personality, capable of development and improvement by the very fact that these emanations are accepted and used continually. When properly used and not abused *in excess,* the power will regenerate itself and the life force, far from being exhausted, will actually increase gradually, especially when psychic vibrations are paired with certain techniques of breathing, meditation exercises, and a generally positive outlook on life itself.

## Chapter IV

# How to Overcome Negative Conditions and See the Results

Essentially mankind is divided into three great groups as far as attitude towards life is concerned. There are those who see everything optimistically, the pollyannas of this world who refuse to acknowledge the existence of evil or bad influences and who will only see that which is good and positive. Then there are those who are born pessimists, who emphasize the negative in life and have little use for the optimist. To the pessimist, anything positive happening or about to happen is nearly one step from disappointment. Whenever the pessimist cannot explain some positive situation away entirely, he will minimize its impact by pointing out that most of that which occurs in this world of ours is negative and destructive. Between these two extremes there is the vast majority of people who accept both positive and negative values as natural and as part of the eternal challenge of life. That, of course, is the only healthy attitude. If everything happening to us were entirely positive and without flaw, then there would be no effort required to cope with it. There would be no challenge, no testing of a person's character and mettle. On the other hand, if all were negative, there would be no hope, no encouragement to try, and that too would be an impossible world.

It must be clearly understood in the context of this work that I do not propose to ignore existing conditions simply because they do not contribute to progress. Negative situations are as valid as positive situations; in fact, sometimes the negative produces greater results than the positive. For example, the continuing warfare in Europe has produced a sharper, more sophisticated culture in general than the culture in some parts of the world which were never touched by warfare, destruction, and suffering. No one can deny that Great Britain and Germany and France, three of the main warfaring countries during the last few centuries, have contributed to many aspects of progress both on the technical and the cultural level. On the other hand, little Switzerland, which has not seen any warfare since the Middle Ages, has found its purpose and fulfillment as a nation in other directions. Adversity is always a character builder, although not necessarily a desirable one. There is another way. Suffering is not a necessity. Feelings of guilt are worthless and man-created. Actions, whether on the physical level or on the mental-emotional-thought level, are all that counts. Since nations are only the sum total of large numbers of individuals and the institutions created and maintained by them, the solution must be found within the individual. How, then, can the average individual overcome negative conditions?

## Overcoming Negative Conditions

A negative condition can be one of two things: It is either the absence of something positive, useful, desired, necessary, or it is the faulty state of something that is essentially positive. By its own definition a negative condition is undesirable, with the sole exception, already noted, that it can sometimes contribute to a strengthening of character in the individual. That, however, is a temporary state of affairs, and prolonged negative conditions do not contribute to character improvement but will inevitably lead to destruction.

The first step to overcome negative conditions is to recognize them. This is not as obvious as it may sound. Many individuals are not even aware of the fact that something in their lives is negative or destructive. For example, take the case of Mr. K.—in good health, in his middle fifties, well educated, and a family man. He has held one position practically all his adult life. He has acquired certain skills even though they are not outstanding. He works in an industry in which there is keen competition for jobs. Nevertheless, his record is fine and he is generally recognized as a man of quality and integrity. Despite this, he has advanced very little in thirty years on the same job. He is too polite to ask for an advancement and too filled with fears of losing his job to try to look elsewhere. In fact, he is so worried that one might hear of his potential interest in a position somewhere else that he has refused to have lunch with anyone working for a competitive company. Does Mr. K. think that his attitude is negative? Not at all. He is firmly convinced that he is prudent and very well off. His wife does not think so. She wants him to try and better himself, to look elsewhere or to make new contacts in his own company, to find a better position for himself after such prolonged and faithful service. But Mr. K. cannot do this because he doesn't agree with his wife's view. What to her seems like a self-imposed form of slavery, a total lack of progress and therefore a negative condition, is to her husband merely a proper satisfactory attitude. Unless Mr. K. recognizes the negative connotation of his position and his relationship to those he works for, he will not be able to do anything about it.

Miss W. is in her middle twenties, works as a secretary in a large eastern city, and is deeply in love with her boss. Her boss, twenty years her senior, is happily married and has given her no reason to hope for a divorce. Nevertheless, Miss W. continues her relationship with her boss even though an outsider, if familiar with the situation, would readily see that it had no future whatsoever. But Miss W. does not want to see her situation in such a light. She does not realize that her relationship with her boss has strong negative aspects. Thus she is unable to leave him and find a better relationship elsewhere. It is impossible for her to change her negative situation, simply because she doesn't recognize it as such.

Mr. F. has suffered from migraine headaches for twenty years. He works in a factory in the state of Pennsylvania and spends most of his working hours in confined, damp, and very noisy quarters. He is fully aware of the fact that his working conditions are less than desirable and has frequently expressed a dislike for his job, but he has never done anything about a change and has continued to stay with the same company. As the years went by, a nagging headache started to develop. When he consulted one doctor after another, he found that no organic cause for his headache could be detected. Eventually he sought out a psychiatrist who subjected him to the usual tests. When the psychiatrist discovered the conflict between the man's desire to change jobs and his inability to do anything about it, he quickly realized that the migraines were caused by this inner conflict. He explained

## Overcoming Negative Conditions

the situation to Mr. F. Unfortunately, Mr. F. did not understand or decided not to accept the theories of psychoanalysis and rejected this explanation as farfetched. He still has his headaches and tries to find an organic cause for them. Although he would like to make a change in his working conditions, he cannot possibly understand how such a problem could in any way influence his nervous system. Thus Mr. F. does not recognize the negative situation in his life either and cannot do anything about it.

Let us assume, however, that the individual who wants to overcome negative conditions in his life does understand them and recognize them as such. The first thing to do is to see if they can be physically altered. If a position is unsatisfactory, one must try and find a better one. If a state of health gives one cause for concern, one must consult with appropriate authorities. If a romantic attachment is a dead-end situation, one must break it off and seek greener pastures. These are obvious directions in which to go and need not be further explained. However, if such direct action is impossible, the individual need not necessarily accept the continuing negative situation as inevitable and hopeless. If the situation itself cannot be changed, then one's attitude towards it must be altered. This concept is based upon a startling fact: Nothing in this world of ours has reality until and unless we become aware of it and relate to it either by our senses or through thoughts. In relating to a person or situation or even an object, our personal attitude is also involved. We relate to a person and either like or dislike him. We relate to a situation by either enjoying it or not enjoying it. We relate to an object by either appreciating it or not appreciating it. In each case, whether it is a relationship between one individual or another individual, situation, or object, there is a personal involvement brought into play as well. Personal involvement means attitude, opinion, view, feelings, thoughts, and reactions. What happens within us is of prime importance to the ensuing result. Our reactions and feelings are much closer to our inner selves than the subject or object of our attention.

Let us take the same three people who have not seen the negative aspects of their situations and assume that they do see the situations as they are in reality. What can they do about them? Mr. K. will suddenly realize the negative aspects of his situation and decide he doesn't like it. However, until such time as he is able to take positive action to alter it, he will accept it as a temporary situation. The first step to overcoming negative situations is to accept them temporarily and to do something about changing them. Meantime, Mr. K. is not going to go into his office in the morning and tell his boss off or tear the papers on his desk and walk out, ego triumphant. He will, however, use all his spare time to make new contacts or improve relations with his own superiors while at the same time performing his duties as well as ever. From that moment on, when his decision has been made to try and alter his conditions, the negative aspects of his current situation will seem less frustrating. As a matter of fact, there will be a certain gusto with which he now applies himself to the job he really hates. He wants to leave in a blaze of glory. As a result, one of two things will happen. Either he will find a more satisfactory position and change jobs, or his sudden zest in a position he has held for thirty years will come to the attention of his superiors and they, in turn, might work Mr. K. into a more satisfactory slot. Either way he gains. Has anything actually changed? Only Mr. K.'s attitude has.

## *Overcoming Negative Conditions*

What about Miss W. and her love for her boss? She recognizes the uselessness of her relationship and mentally frees herself from the ties which have thus far prevented her striking out elsewhere. Suddenly she looks at other men with new eyes. She looks at herself in a different way—not as an attractive woman, but as a free individual capable of attracting someone new and exciting. As a result of this newly found courage, she projects precisely that and before long finds a new and more satisfactory relationship. Has anything changed? Has she changed her makeup, her clothes, her hairdo? Not necessarily. The only thing she has changed is her attitude towards a negative situation. All that time she maintained her friendship with her boss. But there is a difference: She is no longer emotionally dependent upon him. Again, there are two possibilities: She will free herself from his influence the moment someone new appears on the scene, or her less dependent attitude towards her boss and lover spurs his emotions to a point where he must make a decision. If he loves her as much as she loves him, perhaps there will be a divorce and the two might yet get together. Either way, Miss W.'s changed attitude can only result in gains for her.

Mr. F. would also look differently at his migraine headaches if he recognized the connection between his sufferings and his frustrations. In his case the results would be even more dramatic. Immediately upon his realizing the connection between headaches and job frustration, and the firm resolution to do something about it the next morning, the headaches will disappear. Of course, if Mr. F. fails to put into action what he has decided, they will recur, but so long as he is actively engaged in altering his situation he will not suffer from migraine headaches any longer.

## Psycho-Ecstasy

But in addition to recognizing when negative conditions exist and in changing one's attitude towards them, there are two other elements necessary to accomplish the desired results. The third factor involves a proper evaluation of the reasons why negative conditions exist. Most people who are not familiar with my techniques will blame themselves, bad luck, lack of talent or ability, a vengeful God, jealousy, or simply situations beyond their control for the existence of negative conditions in their lives. They will look at them totally negatively in that they see no good whatsoever in such conditions. But every negative condition already contains, within itself, the germ of future positive resolution. The advanced individual will look at these negative situations, and though he may not know what lies ahead in the way of overcoming them, he will somehow feel that they may not have come his way or that he would not have been subjected to these conditions unless they were meant to teach him something. In overcoming, we always learn. Later, in retrospect, we inevitably realize how valuable the negative situation has been in the long pull, even though at the time it happens to us it is totally undesirable and rejected by us. But fate cannot fill a vacancy until one exists. A room filled with air cannot be filled with more air—a vacuum, however, can and will be. To create such a vacuum in our lives is the purpose of negative conditions. Without them, positive conditions cannot take their place.

Mr. A. is a successful attorney in the city of New York. He held a good position with a law firm for several years. Suddenly he was dismissed from his job. He blamed office politics, not understanding the reasons for his dismissal. A week later he met an old friend whom he had not seen for several years. Over lunch Mr. A. was made a proposition

## Overcoming Negative Conditions

involving much travel. It was an exciting and new assignment which he could only accept if he were free to travel. If A. had still been on his job he would have surely rejected this proposition, since he considered his position secure and desirable. Now, however, without a job, he readily accepted and found the new assignment very much more to his liking than the old one had been. If fate had not arranged for him to lose his position and thus create a negative situation, A. would not have been ready to accept the step forward in his career.

The best way to look at negative situations, whether they are in the field of work, personal emotional involvement, health, or otherwise, is to try and eliminate all panic, all irrational attitudes, and to detach oneself as much as possible from the situation as if it were happening to someone else. Calmly looking into the reasons or seeming reasons for the situation to exist, one will then find that despite the essentially negative aspects of it there are already some possible developments included in it and that these positive developments might yet undo the damage done by the negative situation. I am not saying that one should minimize the seriousness of any existing situation, but seriousness is not the same as hopelessness. There is always, or nearly always, a way to cope with undesirable conditions. *There are no bad breaks. There are only good breaks in disguise.* Mr. A.'s being fired was, on the surface at least, a bad break. Finding a better position the following week was certainly a good break. Thus the bad break was really a good break in disguise. And so it goes in many areas of life and with the majority of people, if they will only recognize conditions from that point of view.

A fourth factor to be considered when coping with negative conditions is even more important than the first three.

## Psycho-Ecstasy

Having recognized the existence of a negative situation and changed one's attitude towards it and finally tried to analyze the reasons why such a situation had come about in one's particular case, there still remains the need to apply a positive, outgoing factor, before positive results can be obtained. This is the technique of creating a wish-fulfillment thought in one's own mind and projecting it outward into the world, both at home and when having contact with people in one's field of work or in the area in which one's negative situation lies. The result is sometimes startling.

Mr. J. S. was an assistant producer of a Hollywood daytime serial popularly known as a soap opera. Suddenly he was dismissed from his job. He blamed personal jealousy instead of economics. Had he not been trained in this method of projecting a thought-fulfillment image, he would have been despondent and would have aired his frustrations to anyone willing to listen. Instead, he shrugged and immediately started to build himself a better, more desirable career. He had long wanted to have a leading production job in one of the most important nighttime serials in television. Now he started to project himself as such a person, sending forth the image of himself in the new, desired position, when he was alone as well as when he made the rounds of the offices within his industry. Within a matter of weeks he had made the right contacts and his name was proposed for the position of second in command on that very nighttime program he had wanted to work on. He is now the associate producer of it and far happier than he ever was in his previous position.

A skeptic might say that these four steps, interesting though they are, will not make a broken leg whole or cure an incurable physical affliction. The skeptic is wrong, even though these four steps in overcoming negative conditions are

## Overcoming Negative Conditions

primarily on the personality level of the individual and deal with physical conditions only in a secondary and indirect way. There are, in addition to the four steps, invisible but very tangible psychic forces set in motion by their application that can and will alter the process of healing. It is a medical fact that a positive attitude and expectancy towards healing will make a patient get well that much faster. Projecting a positive force never hurts and can only bring positive results. No matter what, the one who applies this technique will be no worse off than he would be if he did not know of it. Very likely, he will be much better off if he applies it correctly. The results may well be startling.

## Chapter V

# The Second Self

It is a long way from wanting to do something to doing it. Many people may be convinced that a certain course of action should be taken but somehow cannot get themselves to put into objective reality that which they are convinced should be done. This isn't just cowardice. It has nothing to do with being inhibited or introverted. Some of the most outspoken, most aggressive extroverts also find it difficult to do that which they think they ought to do. The gap between conviction, resolution, and action is a real problem to a large percentage of ordinary, well-adjusted people. "I can't get myself to do it," is a phrase frequently heard when someone cannot quite bridge the gap between his convictions and the action he knows he should and must take to overcome a given situation or to obtain a certain goal.

## Psycho-Ecstasy

It starts early in childhood when a child somehow cannot say "thank you" after it has been given a piece of candy. He or she knows that "thank you" are the proper words and that she is expected to use them, but something within her rebels and the words rarely come out. Yet it would have been so simple to say "thank you" and make everyone happy.

As we grow up other situations enter our lives where this gap becomes even more pronounced. In adolescence we frequently find it difficult to express ourselves, especially when certain actions are involved. The teenager who would like to ask a pretty girl to the school dance somehow cannot get himself to go and do it. If he finds within himself the energy and relaxed attitude to go through with it, he would find that the girl would have been most eager to accept him, but something within him prevents him from doing it. Yet, at the same time, he can advise his best friend in a similar matter and find no difficulty in visualizing himself in his friend's shoes, but that is another matter since it is not he who must take the "fatal step" but someone else.

As a person grows older and incipient relationships become more pronounced and significant it is even more difficult to ask someone out for a date, for dinner or perhaps to share some artistic experience with him. Once the ice is broken there are no further difficulties, but it is usually the initial step that cannot be taken.

To be sure, in his mind the young man has it all figured out: He can hear himself saying what he wants to say and he sees a girl react the way he would like her to react. But when the scene is taken from his imagination and put onto the plane of reality, something happens and he can't go through with it. In his professional life he may have a similar situation. He would like to ask the boss for a raise. He knows he deserves it and it is long overdue. He also feels the boss will not refuse him and there isn't any serious problem except one—he can't get himself to do it. Now some people are very aggressive about their aims and desires and they will sound off about them even to strangers. They exteriorize their wishes with such a potent force that by the time they are actually faced with putting them into practice very little steam is left and the entire project fizzles. To a majority of people the act of asking for something represents difficulties. The ability to receive is also not always pronounced or free from problems. Receiving a gift or a favor involves oneself to the point that a normal, well-adjusted person will feel some sense of obligation in return. Unless one is prepared to return the favor at a future date, the act of receiving becomes troublesome. A person who receives favors and does not give them any further thought as to returning them, or who accepts them without the slightest sense of obligation, is not a well-adjusted person. This is closely connected with the art of proper giving, a subject which I have discussed in some detail in *Charismatics*.

I have said at the outset that courage does not enter the picture at all when you are dealing with the ability to bridge the gap between desired action and objective reality. Not one of the people who have the problem are the least bit *afraid* of addressing the other person or making the specific request which they have been able to do in their own minds. None of the questions or requests are the least bit unusual, immoral, or otherwise difficult to accept. The gap between the decision to implement and implementation almost always involves ordinary functions that should not represent any difficulties whatsoever. This frustrating position is accentuated by a highly nervous state during the period when the action could be taken but the individual is not taking it.

I remember when I was a teenager I had great difficulties in asking strange girls to dance with me at school dances or other social functions where asking a strange girl to dance was part of the social structure. Asking for a dance was in no way a violation of the code under which I then lived, nor would it come as a surprise or a shock to the one being asked. On the contrary, it was an expected move and would generally be welcomed. Nevertheless, I would frequently intend asking a certain girl, visualizing myself getting up from my table and walking over to her requesting a dance, but something within me made me hesitate long enough to allow some other fellow to do just that. As soon as I saw that the intended dance partner was no longer free to dance with me, I would sigh with relief and decide that it just wasn't meant to be. At the very last moment, towards the end of the evening, I would finally muster up enough courage to actually go over to the girl with whom I had wanted to dance all evening. At this point, one of two things would happen. Either she would be free to dance with me and would do so, or I would again be too late. If I would actually succeed in having a dance with her, follow-up action would no longer be necessary since it was the last dance of the evening. Having done it once would satisfy my sense of action while at the same time relieving me from any further need to attempt similar action with the same or other girls I would care to dance with. If I was too late again, then I would assure myself that I had done everything within my power to make the attempt and had simply failed. As soon as the final dance had been played and people started to go home, the pressure

## The Second Self

and nervousness left me; and though I felt saddened by my failure, I was nevertheless relieved to know, for that night at least, that I did not have to bridge the gap again.

People will sometimes make outlandish excuses why they should undertake certain actions or why they could not undertake them even though they thought they should. Asking the boss for a raise when a raise is overdue can be a tortuous undertaking if the person who must do the asking doesn't really like to do it. He will start to walk up to his boss and stop halfway as soon as he sees someone else talking to him, or he will look at his boss and notice that he looks pale today and immediately withdraw because he wouldn't want to go to his boss when the latter isn't feeling well. He will find some very tenuous excuse why he cannot go through with his scheme. I have already explained that this has nothing to do with lack of courage nor has it anything to do with fear of failure, even though on the surface it seems to look that way. My refusal to get up from my table and walk across the dance floor to ask a stranger for a dance seems to be motivated by the fear of being rejected by her. No one likes to be rejected in one's quest. But common sense dictates a degree of failure in everyone's life. Thus my expectation that every girl I would ask for a dance would immediately and enthusiastically accept could never be borne out. I knew very well that somewhere along the line I would be turned down and did not take this too personally, since tastes differ between people. The fellow who asked his boss for a raise is fully aware of the possibility of being turned down for reasons not known to him. It might have been an economic problem, or perhaps the boss does not think as highly of him as the employee imagines, or perhaps he has other intentions at the moment when the question is put to him. Failure is always a possibility, but it is neither permanent nor fatal. The important thing is not to succeed but to make the effort. Unfortunately, the gap between deciding to make it and making it is very real. *It* is often the cause of failure and not just fear of failure.

If this problem is very real and often agonizing in the case of ordinary and justified quests, how much more difficult would it be to put into action a demand or intention that is decidedly out of the ordinary? The girl who would like to break off with her boyfriend for good and sound reasons but somehow cannot find a way of doing it is in a position of this kind. He has taken her to expensive restaurants and theaters and has done everything to make her comfortable, and it is precisely at the end of such an evening when she must tell him that she doesn't wish to see him again. This is entirely against good manners and against her inner promptings in terms of propriety and gratitude, but she also knows that she must take this opportunity to end the relationship. She knows what she must do but she cannot bridge the gap, and again the action is not taken. Feebly she agrees to see the man again and the necessary action is postponed.

The executive who has just taken over a new position in which he becomes his best friend's superior suddenly is faced by the necessity of firing his friend. In the interest of the company he must do so but he finds this a distasteful and difficult task. In his heart he knows that he cannot avoid it, but bridging the gap between that conviction and putting it into motion will create difficulties for him.

In this day of permissiveness many a young man, or perhaps even a young woman, would like to be frank with a member of the opposite sex. How do you tell someone you have just met that you want to go to bed with him or her?

## The Second Self

Yet that is what they would like to do and that is what they feel is the honest thing to say. Their upbringing does not stand in the way. Their social convictions do not prevent them from expressing themselves thus freely and unashamedly. But there is something other than these factors that makes it impossible for them to voice their perfectly legitimate and natural desires.

There are two ways of coping with these common, widespread problems. One, of course, is to take the individual who has the problems and work with him or her through psychoanalysis or hypnosis to find out whether there might not be some quirk in the personality that needs attention. This is an intricate and sometimes drawn-out process requiring patience, knowledge of the other individual, and much experimentation. The majority of people do not have access to such help. There is, however, a second method which I have found to be enormously effective and which has the advantage that it does not require the direct help of another person.

The "second self" is simply the creation of an auxiliary personality within oneself. If you have a middle name, give it that name. The second personality must be visualized regularly and seriously as your other twin. He or she looks exactly as you do, has the same tastes, likes and dislikes, but there is one important difference between your twin and you: Anything you want to do but cannot get yourself to do, your twin can accomplish with ease. Your twin has no problems exteriorizing and setting into motion that which is desired by your common mind. Don't forget that your twin and you inhabit the same body. Your twin is also part of you and you are part of your twin, but you have difficulties your twin does not share and your twin has abilities you do not possess. Your twin, in other words, is omnipotent while you are merely human. Thus you are relieved of the necessity of overcoming your human weakness. All you have to do is ask your twin to do it. Your twin has no such difficulty, since there are no problems he or she cannot overcome by merely deciding to do so. You accept your twin as completely independent when it comes to taking actions, but also as an integral part of you once the results are in. Thus you benefit from the results without having to do much about the way these results are gained.

After visualizing your twin as your other self, looking and acting precisely as you do, you must refer to your twin as if you were addressing another person outside of you. Address your twin by your middle name. If you don't have a middle name, invent one. Order your twin about the way the master or mistress orders a servant about, but at the same time do it lovingly so that the relationship between you and your twin is one of friendship and mutual respect. Do not mistake this for an attempt at stripping off part of your personality. You are not creating schizophrenic hazards. There are no dangers in this method, since you are merely visualizing part of yourself in a more favorable light as far as abilities are concerned. If you find that you desire a certain course of action and encounter the usual difficulties of putting your desires into objective reality, do not press the issue. Merely summon your twin by name, in a loud voice if at all possible, and order your twin to take the necessary action. Since you are also cohabiting the same body you will partake of the action as a silent or passive partner watching as your twin goes about his or her work. Gradually, as you practice this method, you will find that you have succeeded in polarizing

## The Second Self

two basic aspects of your personality—your outer self and the face you present to the world will be crystalized in your usual self, but your inner desires and usually your more emotional self will begin to reside in your twin. It is interesting to note that in astrology we also deal with two basic aspects: The actual sign of the Zodiac under which we are born and the so-called rising sign or ascendant. While the sun or Zodiac sign deals with the personality we show to the world, the rising sign generally represents our inner selves and the deeper levels of consciousness.

The second self is not a gimmick. It is not tampering with the unconscious in such a way as to endanger one's sanity or to enhance neurotic conditions. It is a little like a spark plug in a car. A spark plug by itself cannot drive a car but is very necessary to set fire to the gasoline inside the motor, so that in exploding under controlled conditions, the driving force is generated. With the second self there is no possible failure. Consequently, doubts or negative emotions concerning the future of one's actions and other deterrent factors are totally absent in this technique. Instead, a comfortable feeling of expectancy and a very positive outlook are created. If you are still plagued by guilt feelings, which anyone not familiar with my charismatic techniques may harbor, you will find that the second self also takes care of the problem of guilt. Since all actions are the work of another individual, so to speak, there can be no guilt feeling for oneself. As for the second self feeling guilty, that is also impossible since it is omniscient and omnipotent and therefore cannot create states of failure or guilt. Anyone who is always right cannot possibly be wrong. The second self is your invisible partner in every aspect of life. It is important to realize that we have the ability to exteriorize such a second self from within us and make the twin do our bidding. By so doing we begin to create the conditions which make higher developments of ourselves possible. The twin eliminates a large number of everyday frustrations by simply making us do the things we thought we could not do. Only good can come from it.

## Chapter VI

# The Nature of Love

Perhaps one of the most abused words in today's language is the word *love*. In addition to its traditional usage it is nowadays a political slogan. Young rebels advise us to make love, not war. Various faiths ask that we do things in the name of love. The advertising profession reminds us that we should love this or that product. The classical and perhaps most basic book on love relations ever written, *The Art of Loving* by Eric Fromm, reminds us that we must first love ourselves before we can expect to love another person or be loved by another person. It also teaches us that it is not enough to fall in love but that we must learn to stay in love to make such a relationship meaningful. I have always advised anyone experiencing emotional problems or going through stages of immaturity to study this work by the eminent psychiatrist.

What exactly is love? Broadly speaking, it is a positive relationship involving some form of attraction between two individuals, or between one individual and an object, idea, place, or other entity. What many people do not realize is the fact that love is not simply an attitude alone. When there is a love feeling between individuals or an individual and some other entity, something passes between them. Love between people is, of course, of the highest order. Small particles of energy imprinted with the emotional impulses of one or both people pass between them, and in this way strengthen their relationship. Love is impossible without a thought process going on at the same time, but this is not a logical form of thinking. There is, as we already know, a higher form of thinking which I have called emotional thinking. This process involves a wave of feeling going out from oneself, a feeling which is certainly defined in its nature and context, but not in the way a mathematical formula is defined. Emotional thoughts differ from logical thoughts precisely the way a painting differs from a photograph. Both are necessary and useful in the proper context; however, when we are dealing with emotional thoughts we are dealing with the essence of personality. Purely logical thoughts need not involve one's own views or feelings, since logic is objective and quite natural, whereas emotional thinking is personal and subjective.

There are many kinds of love. First of all, there are love relationships between child and parent, between relatives, between friends. Then, on the next higher level of human consciousness, there is the love relationship between lovers of opposite sexes. Their union represents the highest form of human consciousness and involves the opening wedge to psychic awareness, as we shall see later on.

In interpersonal relationships there are also love relationships not sanctioned by society, but which nevertheless represent a genuine love feeling on the part of one or both parties: These are the homosexual syndrome, the incest syndrome, and other forms of deviation. Then, of course, there are love relationships between people and ideas. And the missionary love which represents the relationship between oneself and one's profession, one's calling, one's goal, or one's country, when it is called patriotic love, and the quasi-religious love in which the religious symbol, whether it is Christ, God, or some other deity, replaces the human partner who, for one or the other reason, cannot be found. All these are love relationships in the true sense of the term because feelings go out from the emotional center of one person towards another or towards the outside world. Here also belongs the love of things such as fine art, treasures, buildings, and symbolic representatives of ideas one loves, and finally the love between man and animal.

One of the great difficulties of today is the difficulty of separating "love" from "sex." We live in a strongly sex-oriented and sex-motivated society in which many of the old taboos have fallen by the wayside. As a result of this fairly sudden upheaval, undue emphasis has sometimes been placed on the sexual aspects of the love relationship to the detriment of the more deeply involving emotional factor. A true love relationship between individuals of the opposite sex is impossible without sexual relations. A sex relationship between two people is, however, entirely feasible without a *permanent* love relationship. However, it is my contention that even in the case of casual sexual relationship some love

## Psycho-Ecstasy

has to enter the picture even if it is of fleeting duration. At the moment of desire a love impulse does go back and forth between the two parties and this thought factor is greatly responsible for the satisfactory completion of sexual intercourse. Much of the disappointment so frequently found in modern marriages stems from the absence of the love factor in sexual relationships.

Love factors cannot be manufactured at will nor can they be forced. They are built from a number of intangibles in the relationship. It has been the traditional view that a "chemical reaction" starts the process towards a love-fulfillment relationship. I contend that the opposite is true. The love relationship starts in a number of ways in which the two potential partners find they are compatible. There is a common bond in professional life, art, music, nature, or perhaps only in the way in which one looks at the world. There may be casual phrases spoken between them that create emotional thought waves from one to the other. If there is any physical contact at all at the beginning it may be only a slight touch of the hand or it may be a look at the potential partner's face or into his or her eyes. Strong contact can be made from eye to eye, as I have already pointed out in *Charismatics*. What has happened to make the two people aware of each other from the onset was not a chemical reaction but *attraction*, pure and simple. It was an undefinable, subtle, but very definite feeling of wanting to be with the other person and to learn more about him or her. *At the end* of the relationship stands the chemical reaction. The culmination of their love relationship, whether it be inside or outside of marriage, will lead to sexual relationship and the union that produces total fulfillment. That, then, is a biochemical process completing that which was started at the beginning when a state of

## The Nature of Love

attraction between the two individuals initiated the entire love process.

There are rare instances where the direction of the flow is reversed. That is to say, where a sudden sexual attraction is followed by gradual deeper love involvement. Generally the flow works the other way around in an ascending curve and it usually maintains its level of awareness and involvement for long periods. The duration of these periods differs with individuals, and will depend largely upon the number of focal points the two share: A common philosophy and outlook, similar interests, mutual respect, mutual participation in each other's professional activities, periodical changes in routines and way of life—all are contributing factors to a long and enduring love relationship. These factors, in turn, increase and improve the purely biochemical, sexual aspects of the relationship as well. It is the thought—and the feeling within the thought—behind the action that makes the action significant and enjoyable.

If the direction of the love relationship has proceeded from the attraction stage to the culmination in sexual union, then future sexual relationships will either maintain the high level of consciousness and involvement or increase it beyond the initial stage. This is contrary to the development in many ordinary relationships where there is a gradually declining curve of emotional attachment in these relationships as time goes on. Greater familiarity with the partner lessens the impact and consequently the interest.

Although not quite love relationships, there are three states of mind bordering on love: They are sympathy, empathy, and compassion. Sympathy is the feeling of kinship with someone undergoing an emotional stress or a situation requiring understanding and perhaps help. We may also sympathize with a cause, which means that our thoughts concerning it run parallel to the thoughts of others actively engaged in supporting that cause, without, however, necessitating any action on our part. A sympathetic person is someone you like without necessarily loving him or her. Sympathetic merely means that you can have dialogue with that person, or that his or her presence in your immediate vicinity creates harmonious feelings.

Empathy differs from sympathy in the way you yourself are involved. You may feel empathy towards a cause without agreeing with it. It may be a just cause, although you yourself feel differently about the same issue and your position is simply one of supporting the right of the other party to their view. Empathy requires a great degree of tolerance. At the same time, empathy does not require personal or emotional involvement on your part, and it might even involve your giving a platform or an opportunity to be heard to someone—or to a cause—with which you disagree. The principle of empathy, then, is to allow opposites to be heard and to allow views to be expressed with which one may or may not identify oneself.

Compassion, finally, represents a deep personal concern for another person or a cause one wishes to extend help to without necessarily identifying with it. Compassion is a deeper emotion than sympathy, but it involves less of one's own commitment than sympathy does. When you sympathize with someone or a cause, you are in accord with him or it. When you have compassion for someone you may be totally divorced from what he or his cause stands for, but you nevertheless want to help him or his cause simply because you respect his commitment to the cause. Compassion comes into force particularly when a positively oriented

## The Nature of Love

person is faced with a negative individual, when hatred or destructive tendencies are to be dealt with. To hate one's enemies is wrong. To have compassion for them is a proper attitude. Compassion is not the same as pity. Pity involves simply looking down upon another individual without any constructive feeling. When there is compassion there is genuine concern, and there are elements present indicating one's desire to help the other person see the light. With pity it is simply an attitude and nothing more. But compassion for the other person does not require action on your part. It means one may express one's opinion, one's suggestions may be heard and a hand extended. If the suggestions are not taken and the hand grasped, one's obligation really ceases. Compassion is as much a feeling of self-satisfaction as it is one of extending oneself to another person.

The opposite of love is not hate but a neutral state in which no feelings of affinity whatsoever are expressed. This feeling of emptiness is by no means desirable, and is in a sense more dangerous to mental well-being than the hate feeling. Total absence of any love relationship in one's life may very well create mental and emotional imbalance and deprive the individual of a sense of purpose, thus creating the beginnings of mental and emotional disintegration. Hate, on the other hand, far from being the opposite of love, is actually closely related to love. It is simply the negative expression of the same feeling exteriorized in love. One can turn into the other sometimes quickly and easily. It is a well-known fact that a rejected lover frequently turns to hating the erstwhile subject of his affection. Imagined or real hurts, jealousy, frustration and rejection can all change a love feeling into a hate feeling. The more intense the love feeling has been the greater the hate will be. Hate parallels whatever feelings and feeling-motivated actions one has undertaken towards a love relationship. It is possible to change the positive or love force into the negative or hate force through such simple actions as verbal expressions, or even the absence of expected communication. Of course, negative or hate feelings can be upgraded to positive or love feelings by a number of methods: Verbal stimulation by choosing the proper phrase, rationalization, and artificial stimuli through certain benign drugs. Finally, extrasensory means and unorthodox healing have also frequently been employed to change such an attitude, as has hypnotherapy in extreme cases.

The love-hate syndrome does not only apply to individual relationships. It is of even greater concern when one escalates individual relationship, into the relationships between nations, between political parties, between groups of social or economic nature, between professional groupings, in fact, across the entire range of human activities. The energies used to nourish hate feelings can be used in a constructive way to create a love bond. While these energies are totally useless in the hate expression they can be very valuable to cement better relationships, or to be actively creative, especially in a professional sense. There are a few unusual exceptions to this rule, such as hate feelings expressed towards a patently negative force—a political tyrant, an evil person, an oppressive situation. In that case the hate force becomes the driving force to change things for the better.

Perhaps the love-hate syndrome is best explained if one points out that deep inside even the most harmonious love relationship there slumbers the seed of destruction. The potential hate impulse is always present and a primitive expression of the fear of losing one's love object. In most harmonious love relationships this never comes to the surface. It

## The Nature of Love

becomes an issue only if there is doubt in the relationship, disloyalty, or outright enmity between the two partners for one reason or another. But it is natural for one person to fear the loss of the other's love. Only the rare and very advanced individual will react to such a loss with a sense of sorrow and acceptance. The majority of individuals, however, will react with anger.

The loss of love represents not only rejection of self but also the loss of something valuable, something one has cherished; thus it is a double disappointment. At the very deep level of consciousness where this potential hate syndrome resides, the emotional, mental and physical portions of ourselves are well-integrated. If the love-hate syndrome becomes activated into its negative aspect, it will therefore become prominent on all three levels: On the mental level, love turning into hate will express itself in verbalization; on the emotional level, in a desire to hurt the former love object; and on the physical level, the change into hate may manifest itself in the rejection of those physical attributes one has until then cherished in the love object by turning to the opposite, by turning quickly to what is popularly called "rebound love," and in general using one's physical love ability in directions that are totally different from the one experienced before love turned to hate.

It is true that animals, especially the higher kind and those who have become pets of man, are capable of feelings similar to love. However, these feelings are primitive and do not attain the multilevel expression only man is capable of. Thus it appears that one of the principle characteristics of man is his ability to express love. Perhaps love is that divine spark put into man that raises him above the animal level and makes him a distinct species in nature. If man was created in

## Psycho-Ecstasy

God's image and God is love, then perhaps that is so. But the absence of love certainly makes man less than what nature intended him to be. Only through love does man finally express himself and only in love can man reach the height of fulfillment as an individual put into nature for a definite purpose. Anyone wishing to rise to higher levels of consciousness through psychic methods or other forms of mind expansion must first fully realize the need to develop his capabilities to love and be loved.

## Chapter VII
# Ecstasy: The Left-Hand Path

What exactly is ecstasy? The word itself is derived from the Greek. 'Ec' means outside or going outside or going beyond, and 'stasy' is the anglicized version of the Greek word for condition or state of being. Ecstasy, then, means an extraordinary state of being. But in modern terms ecstasy refers to a pleasant sensation. Thus, one can be in an extraordinary state and be extremely unhappy. That, of course, does not constitute ecstasy. Ecstasy is perhaps best explained as a state of altered consciousness in which the individual experiences certain emotional stimuli—visions, feelings, sounds, colors, smells and other forms of sensory perceptions—which are different from those experienced under ordinary conditions. As a result of ecstasy the subject is

## Psycho-Ecstasy

removed from the three-dimensional world of reality, without, however, being able to define in precise terms the dimension into which his ecstatic state has catapulted him.

Ecstasy in religious terms is usually reserved for priests, saints, or highly evolved individuals for whom the religious experience constitutes a major factor in their lives. Average people never experience religious ecstasy. To the casual observer, anyone experiencing religious ecstasy seems to be possessed by the deity and inspired by knowledge and guidance beyond human ability. Thus the ecstatic preacher is thought to be a direct link to God. To be chosen for such a task indicates a great deal of merit on the part of the vehicle, and for that reason ecstatic priests were considered to be demigods and worshiped like saints. This even included some cases where the ecstatic behavior was clearly due to personality maladjustments, hallucinations, illusions, or physical ailments such as epilepsy. The devout might, of course, argue that such states of seeming illness were in fact induced by God to create a receptive condition in the individual through whom the divine message was to be channeled. But to the orthodox scientist they also represent possible rational explanations for otherwise inexplicable behavior, and for some of the fantastic material that has sometimes come out of the mouths of certain ecstatic religious personalities.

Religious ecstasy is also a oneness with God, or with nature if one is a follower of a nature cult. In the ecstatic state the entire physical body seems more vibrant and more open to influences from outside than under ordinary circumstances; the mind is particularly clear and the emotional state is one of extreme exhilaration. In this state one truly experiences the creative joy of being one with the godhead. Depending upon the individual and his abilities to respond to these stimuli, he will have vivid, intensely personal experiences different from anyone else's even under the same conditions, experiences which are difficult to explain in ordinary language. Even after the state of ecstasy has ceased for such an individual, the memory of it will leave behind a state of beatitude or serenity in which ordinary conditions, difficulties, hindrances and human problems assume small proportions and no longer represent threats to the individual's well-being.

Seeking religious ecstasy is probably the highest form of expressing one's faith in a desire to come close to the deity. There is no certain way of reaching it or training for it, so to speak, but an attitude of deep emotional involvement in all religious ritual will be the proper setting for spontaneous ecstasy to occur.

Creative ecstasy is another form of reaching out from the ordinary state of being. This is particularly important to artists, writers and others in creative professions—people who depend upon ideas as their tools or as their guiding inspirations. No one really knows where ideas come from. The materialistic point of view has them originate in the brain of man by some darkly understood biochemical process. The metaphysician prefers to say that ideas come from a world mind into which one can, so to speak, plug one's own thoughts and thus derive information of a creative nature for oneself. From my own experiences I can only state that the creative process in man is one of the most complex and most unique processes within life, and that it involves more than one factor.

Certainly, a creative thought does come into being within man's personality. It is his own doing whether through biochemical processes within his body or by thought processes

## Psycho-Ecstasy

or by a combination of both. Possibly a third factor, emotional in nature, may also be involved. However, outside influences may stimulate this creative process. It is my observation that creative ideas have come into being that could not have occurred within the individual who brought them to the attention of the world. They may well be the result of discarnate influence by someone who does have the creative spark within him, although he is no longer in the physical body. I think creative processes are an inter-play of individual human endeavor guided and sometimes sparked by discarnates, humans on the other side of life, for purposes of contributing ideas. The discarnates, still wishing to contribute ideas initiated in their physical state, try to give the world something they feel the world should have at a certain point.

Creative ecstasy occurs when the individual creative person has reached a state of excellence or perfection in his work that seems to surmount the usual norm. A particularly well done painting might induce in the painter a state of creative ecstasy. A musical composition of enormous emotional impact could lead its composer to believe that he has reached a unique state of ecstasy in which he has accomplished the expression of his talent in a particularly fortuitous way. Creative ecstasy then, in a professional sense, means a unique expression of individual talent way above the ordinary, faultless, at least to the creator, and likely to be of major impact to others than the creator. Every artist and writer hopes someday to reach the state of creative ecstasy if only for one moment. The benefit of having reached that zenith of knowledge will be with him for the rest of his life.

Related to creative ecstasy, but of a different kind, is the ecstatic state reached because of excellence in one's chosen profession, in one's calling, in one's mission in life. This, unfortunately, also includes the ecstasy of power. In some cases the state of power ecstasy is reached when the individual leaves behind all sense of proportion and reason and becomes what we call "power mad."

Although ecstasy as such is a positive factor, it can in the case of power madness turn into a negative force. We have seen this happen throughout history in the case of despots and mad dictators.

The fact that one has accomplished one's mission in life, even if it is only success in a business, can lead to an ecstatic feeling about one's work. It is not the same emotional uplift as with the religious ecstatic or the creative ecstatic experiences. A much quieter sense of ecstasy, it is nevertheless nearly as rewarding as the other two are. Very few people reach the zenith of professional ecstasy in the non-creative fields. Perhaps Albert Schweitzer is a good case in point, or Albert Einstein.

Sexual ecstasy is even more difficult to reach than the other states. Almost everyone engaging in a love relationship or even in a non-love relationship hopes to reach that state. But sexual ecstasy depends on several factors: first of all, the right partners, and then their inter-relationship on many levels—physical, mental, emotional, philosophical, religious, professional, in artistic tastes, likes and dislikes. Each of these factors may ruin the relationship and rob the couple of reaching sexual ecstasy. Since the culmination of the sexual act requires total union between the two participants it also requires a union of outlook. At the moment of culmination the two individuals feel entirely as one. Sexual ecstasy occurs when the two individuals rise together above the physical state into a state of beatitude released from physical ties. It is odd that physical means are used to release human beings

## Psycho-Ecstasy

from the physical relationship, but the state of ecstasy reached under these conditions is far more fulfilling than the merely physical state can be. Unfortunately, it is the exception rather than the rule. People find, by and large, that it is difficult to agree in some of the areas that seem to be important to the reaching of this state of union and they will look for ways of smoothing over differences and reaching total union with the help of artificial stimulation.

Ordinarily people experience various moods in a changing rhythmical pattern. It is entirely abnormal to have no change of mood, but it is completely within the purpose of man's emotional apparatus to be alternating between states of elation and mild depression. When the states of both elation and depression become accentuated we speak of psychoneurotic individuals. To have no curve of mood is as unhealthy as having extreme fluctuations. Beyond elation lies ecstasy. Beyond depression lies disaster. There is no single word to describe the state that occurs when an individual cannot cope with his life. Nothing is of interest, a desperate flight from reality is sought, and almost any means that promises a turn in the opposite direction is welcome.

The lack of lust for life, the lack of interest for anything and everything whether it is attainable or not are some of the crucial elements in this state beyond depression. Perhaps disillusionment is a more appropriate word to describe it. We live in a world of shattered hopes of the future. No one likes to live in such a state for very long. Thus the desirable action is to turn in the opposite direction. At first the disillusioned seek only a neutral state which they can reach by various artificial means such as smoking, alcohol, games, entertainment in the general sense, but the impression weakens soon and a stronger antidote against disillusionment is sought. The

## The Left-Hand Path

next step is to seek out a state of elation. This state can be reached through stronger stimulations: sex, thrills, danger, fast movements such as racing cars, certain sports requiring great physical stamina, games of chance, sometimes cruelty, the infliction of pain on others or on animals, exhibitionism, extremism in dress, loud noises such as rock and roll music. These are all means of reaching states of elation, strange as it may seem. Eventually a moment is reached when even these stimuli no longer suffice to satisfy the craving for excitement which alone promises escape from the deep-seated inner state of disillusionment. Now ecstasy is being sought after. The ultimate state of "getting out of oneself" is the only solution to one's inner turmoil.

In former years the majority of those needing such stimulation turned to excessive amounts of alcohol, to sexual deviation and already to certain rare drugs. When LSD or lysergic acid came into use along with mescaline, peyote, and the better-known common drugs such as marijuana, hashish, cocaine, a sudden new wave of habits was created. In varying degrees and depending again on individual abilities, bodily and mental conditions and other unique factors, people taking these drugs experienced a true state of ecstasy. True, that is, from their point of view, but totally subjective. In the few cases where mediums took small doses of LSD to experience psychic visions the result was of no scientific value. The value of drug stimulation lies totally in the release of the individual from the abyss of disillusionment. Unfortunately, the release is temporary and increasing doses of the drug are necessary to maintain this sublimation. While it lasts, the state of bliss is extreme. All limitations of space or time are removed, and the individual seems to be beyond the laws of nature. There is a continuum between the self and the sur-

## Psycho-Ecstasy

rounding atmosphere. All emotional experiences are multiplied a thousand fold. At the same time all touch with reality is totally lost which makes these states of ecstasy particularly dangerous to the individual if they occur on the street or away from a safe bed. That, however, is not the only danger of drugs. There are permanent damages to the physical apparatus, to the mind and certainly to the emotions. Whenever alien chemical substances are introduced into the bloodstream they create an imbalance of the natural biochemical system. The effect is known to be cumulative and it cannot be reversed. This even holds true for so-called minor drugs such as marijuana which in the opinion of some medical authorities is harmless. If it is harmless in terms of physical damage it certainly is not harmless in relation to emotional and mental states. Marijuana creates a state of disassociation from reality similar to a stupor and indirectly can be dangerous even to the physical self. I have seen various people "stoned" with eyes glazed, sitting there and waiting for the effect to wear off. They were tranquil, relaxed and peaceful all right, but they did not seem to me particularly happy or even remotely ecstatic. Many people use marijuana in lieu of a tranquilizer, which it is not. Even tranquilizers and their opposites, pep pills, are not without danger. For that matter neither is the excessive use of alcohol, coffee or any other stimulants. Used in the ordinary sense, they are generally tolerated. None of these, however, will create a state of ecstasy. Only the so-called hard drugs can do that. It is true that some drugs have always been used in certain religious cults, especially among the American Indians and in India proper. There is also the so-called witchcraft ointment of the Middle Ages which contained hallucinogenic drugs, such as the deadly nightshade and belladonna, used to create illusions of flying through the air.

## The Left-Hand Path

All these external stimulations for the purpose of reaching ecstasy I have called the left-hand path. They are the wrong way to attain this goal because they involve damage to one of the three systems of personality, either the physical, the mental or the emotional, or to all three. Secondly, the ecstasy which they are able to create is not an extension of reality into other dimensions but a divorce from reality, and results in the creation of an imaginary sphere solely dependent upon biochemical reactions within the system of man. In this form of ecstasy no link with the deity is reached, even though it may be attempted. It is my contention that all strong drugs prevent rather than enhance linking up with a godhead. Some of those who take these drugs may imagine themselves to be at peace with God or in oneness with God, but, as their individual personalities have been totally submerged by the drug, they are really in no position to judge that which goes on within them. I am convinced that this is an illusory experience, a false ecstasy which resembles the real ecstasy only in one respect. Both accomplish a "getting out of one's self." The left-hand path gets you out of yourself without going anywhere in particular while the true ecstasy leads to a linking up with a very real dimension beyond ours.

The only artificial stimulus I find useful in reaching ecstasy the right way is incense. The burning of incense purifies the air and creates a higher vibration in the ether. The "stepping-up" of vibrations or electrical impulses in the atmosphere makes that atmosphere more conducive to psychic communication. It also serves to relax those within it and in turn open them up to ecstatic experiences. The burning of incense does not dull the senses in any way. To the contrary, it refreshes and stimulates. There are many kinds of incense and all of them are made from one plant or another.

## Psycho-Ecstasy

Many of those who choose the left-hand path to ecstasy are not even aware of the consequences. Cases abound where people on a "bad trip" are incapable of returning to the normal state. The result may be insanity or suicide. It must be borne in mind that many of those who seek ecstasy do so because they are already incapable of coping with life. They are in a state of disillusionment, and if they descend back into it too quickly from the heights of their artificial ecstasy caused by drugs, they may find themselves far worse off then they were to begin with. At that point all reasoning ceases and pain may be intense. The only out for some may be to end consciousness in the way most people think best, through suicide. Unfortunately for those who have done this, suicide is not the end but merely the beginning of going back to school and learning what they have failed to understand in one lifetime—and perhaps returning in another to undo the damage.

The left-hand path to ecstasy does not lead to ecstasy; it merely leads to a false image of it, and ultimately to self-destruction. I would not be categorical about drugs, alcohol, tobacco, especially when taken in excess, if I didn't know of a better way of reaching the same goal. But the left-hand path does not mix with the right-hand path or with any other approach to ecstasy. It is either one or the other. Bear that in mind if you think that you can have your real ecstasy and still continue with the wrong approaches of the past. Even *occasional* drugs can destroy whatever you build up with the methods I discuss in this work.

## Chapter VIII

# Ecstasy:
# The Right-Hand Path

To reach the state of ecstasy in a constructive, nonviolent, nontoxic way, is, of course, much more difficult. When pursuing the left-hand or negative approach, one need only follow the directions on the bottle, so to speak, and all positive forces that might otherwise stand in the way are simply swamped. The negative force or artificial stimulation is always stronger than the natural positive force within, unless special techniques have been learned. With the right-hand path towards ecstasy we are, of course, aware of interferences from the left-hand side. The interference does not stem from artificial stimulation so much as the temptation to use it. Thus, the first thing necessary to attempt reaching ecstasy by positive natural means is a state of mind in which

## Psycho-Ecstasy

firmness is of paramount importance. From the beginning one must resolve to reject any and all artificial stimulations of the kind described in the previous chapter no matter how strongly one may feel the sudden need for them, no matter how much one might fail in one's attempt to reach ecstasy by the right-hand path. This firm resolve has to be made over and over again, perhaps every morning prior to attempting further approaches towards ecstasy. It should be kept in mind that backsliding will ruin anything accomplished until that moment, and one has to start all over again if such unfortunate regression should occur.

Religious ecstasy by the right-hand path is a rare and often beautiful thing if it does not degenerate into fanaticism. It is necessary to have a clear even if illogical image of the godhead, of the aim one has in one's religious pursuit. People seeking to reach an exalted state of ecstasy in the religious domain will be very special people. They will have given up many of the temptations of the material life, and even if they are not religious professionals—that is to say priests, nuns, or monks, they are oriented differently from the average businessman or professional pursuing a career. Although they may have mundane interests as well, if there is a conflict they will inevitably decide for the religious point of view. Reaching religious ecstasy then becomes a way of life, a goal towards which they must strive, and death of the physical body plays a very small part in it. If they can reach it prior to death all is well and good, but they will accept without struggle God's decision to call them to Him prior to that time if that is in the cards.

There are several ways in which a religiously oriented person may attempt to reach religious ecstasy; through prayer, especially repeated prayer said meaningfully and with deep emotional connotations, through a religious discipline of saying prayers at certain times and on certain occasions and performing rites as we would say colloquially, "religiously," and by verbalizing desires often in impromptu prayers to the deity asking that God grant them the grace of being lifted up into the ecstatic state. Then, too, through fasting and deprivation of the body in order to become more attuned to the spiritual element within. By the act of long periods of sequestration, by what the Catholics call *retreat* or what amounts to living temporarily as a hermit, a man can greatly enhance his religious feelings and come close to being in tune with the deity. During these periods he may very well experience the "being outside himself" feeling which we now know as astral projection but which in earlier times was thought to be an extraordinary supernatural state caused by the deity or God's angels. In astral projection the ties between the body and mind-spirit are loosened, and the inner personality is released temporarily from within the body and may roam at will in the astral sphere.

Another method of reaching out towards ecstasy which was popular in the Middle Ages, and which, hopefully, is no longer practiced today is the inflicting of pain on oneself as through flagellation. During the Middle Ages, especially in the Latin countries such as Spain and Portugal, large groups of monks practiced this rite of hurting themselves in order to attain a sense of exhilaration. Modern psychiatrists have pointed out the close relationship between this peculiar approach to religious ecstasy and the need for sexual stimulation and gratification. During sexual intercourse some people require the infliction of pain as part of their needs. The medieval monk considered the process of flagellation punishment for the sins of the world including his own and enjoyed the opportunity of atoning for them. In this way, more or less intellectually motivated, the medieval monk hoped to attain ecstasy.

Other ways towards religious ecstasy involve singing and dancing, and music in general. In the temples of the Eastern religions there have always been temple dancers and temple musicians. Together with the burning of strong incense, these stimulations can create in the worshipper a state of suspension from the physical world during which he meditates or on rare occasions rises to reach out to the upper levels of consciousness where man's own expanded mind-world touches upon the sphere of the deity. Even in mundane ways the elements of the dance and music have pronounced effects upon the state of the personality.

Drums and other percussion instruments also play an important role in many primitive religions. Continued drum beat creates a state of somnambulism in which the seeker finds himself in a state of acuteness in which he reaches out to the religious experience somewhat in the manner a person under the influence of a psychedelic drug may experience an unusual state of mind. Sound has long been recognized as a primary source of emotional stimulation. Specific sights can have similar effects, although not as prominently. The flickering display of many candles in church, the reflected glow of light from multicolored church windows are intended as agents of stimulation. The scent of incense, of various aromatics, and even of the burning candles are all calculated to stimulate certain elements in man which tend to lead him towards the religious experience. These, however, are not by themselves capable of lifting him up into the realms of true ecstasy. They are merely primary factors to create a more religious state of mind at the beginning of the desired experi-

## The Right-Hand Path

ence. Somewhere towards the middle of his attempt to reach ecstasy he will become totally attuned to the surroundings in which he finds himself, whether it is an actual temple or church or his own home.

At this point, when his ordinary senses are somewhat lulled, the proper incantation or prayer may very well lift him up into the higher realms of ecstasy. It is difficult to say what will work for each individual person but a combination of all the above-named factors certainly helps greatly towards accomplishing this goal. In the long run, the religious ecstasy experience depends largely upon the individual personality and the degree to which he or she will identify with the need to reach that exalted state.

On the mundane level ecstasy may very well be reached in many professions or business pursuits. Any individual who truly believes in his calling in an almost missionary sense and accomplishes at some time in his life a zenith of success may experience at that moment something akin to ecstasy. George L. is a commercial artist in Philadelphia. Despite his great artistic talent he was never able to succeed as an academic painter despite the fact that he had desired such success more than anything else. In his middle twenties he therefore turned to commercial art and became affluent and respected in this field, working for one of the larger advertising agencies in his city. But the dream of eventually accomplishing recognition as a painter never died within him. Whenever he could he took time out to work on a certain mural which he had erected in the barn of his country place not far from the city. He carefully guarded this barn from outsiders, jealously refusing to show his future work to anyone, not even his own family. After twelve years the mural was finished. With the proper flourish he then invited the entire art community, the

## Psycho-Ecstasy

press and his friends to be present at the unveiling of the mural. The subject of his work had to do with an early visionary experience involving the Last Supper. Thus, in a parallel to Leonardo's famous painting of the same subject, George unveiled his own version of the Last Supper to a surprised and delighted audience. The spontaneous reaction of this group, which included the real leaders of his world, was so strong it caused a most unusual and unexpected reaction within George. At the height of the applause and as people reached out to shake his hand in congratulation, he found himself strangely removed from the scene as if there was a wall between his skin and his inner self.

Although he kept on shaking hands he felt nothing, but instead he experienced the most unusual sense of soaring up into the clouds while at the same time keeping his feet on the ground. For about three or four minutes his physical body continued to function normally even though he later did not recall a single word that either he or others had said. But he does recall very vividly that he found himself, simultaneously near the painting and in a kind of cloud chamber surrounded by various undescribable colors and sound effects he had never heard before, or since. He experienced, at the same time, a strong feeling of uplift and an urge of wanting to cry and laugh at the same time. His feelings of extreme ecstasy lasted only for a few minutes but in his memory it will last him a lifetime. It had not been expected. It had not been planned but it happened spontaneously at a moment when all was right for it to happen, drawing of course upon the accumulated energies of all those years he had spent preparing himself for that moment.

Sometimes political leaders may experience a sense of ecstasy if they truly believe in the justice of their cause. At the height of their oratory they may find themselves quite literally "carried away" by the power of their own words. They are at the same time no longer choosing those words, as it were, but being guided by a higher intelligence. The audiences refer to the speaker as being inspired. The late great attorney, Clarence Darrow, famed for his many appearances on behalf of unpopular causes, such as in the case of the Scopes Trial (or "Monkey Trial") of Tennessee, had the gift of rising above the mundane on such occasions. Speakers, political or otherwise, who can reach out into the rarified sphere of ecstasy will frequently sway audiences away from causes or into new causes overriding any and all objections of critics, logical restraint or anything else that may interfere with the acceptance of their words. In ecstasy man is the nearest thing to God he ever can be. He is not God himself but God dwells within him to the degree that each individual is capable of housing the deity. Ecstasy can never be a permanent state of being but must of necessity be interrupted by long periods of functioning at an ordinary level. If this were not so man could not continue to live with the body and mind nature has given him. He would burn himself out rapidly and the very purpose of ecstatic exaltation would then be lost.

Sexual ecstasy is not what the average reader may think it implies. Merely to reach an orgasm does not represent sexual ecstasy, but it is one of the components if properly controlled. Above all, sexual ecstasy requires total, simultaneous love ecstasy. The imagery of the desired love partner being in total union with oneself must proceed the actual act. Ordinarily very few people reach this state, especially not at the same time as the partner. Reams have been written on the subject of sexual fulfillment. Some books contain the advice

## Psycho-Ecstasy

that the non-physical elements in a relationship must be stressed simultaneously with the physical elements. Actually there are no strict divisions between physical and nonphysical; they flow into each other and are both of the same energy-mass material all creation is made of. But it is essential, if one is to reach sexual ecstasy at times, that one prepare oneself very carefully through proper imagery, proper feeling towards the love object or partner and through various steps of self-purification. Outer conditions are very important too: lack of pressure or any kind of nervous tension, total privacy, and a certain sense of timelessness whereby one is assured of divorcement from the mundane conditions.

Reaching sexual ecstasy through the right-hand path is most desirable but very difficult to accomplish. The new techniques described by me in the following chapters may produce this state more easily than the ordinary, arduous path will. This is so because extreme discipline is required to accomplish it by natural positive means and the slightest disturbance whether mental or physical can throw the result off. The harmony between the two partners is of primary importance. Unfortunately, such total harmony rarely exists between love partners. They may think they have this precious gift but in retrospect often discover they have no such bond but were merely hoping for it. In a small number of cases sexual ecstasy can be reached accidently, and sometimes deliberately, by two completely perfect mates following these or similar instructions towards their goal. Invariably, a love relationship of great depth must also coexist with it. When that state is reached the two individuals function entirely as one unit both in a sensory and in an emotional way, and for a few brief moments experience a state of total

## The Right-Hand Path

bliss in which they are not conscious of earthly limitations. In this state their senses are totally satisfied and a strong feeling of detachment will fill them with a kind of joy that is at once self-contained and overflowing. They will not dare to move out of fear of breaking the spell of the state they have just attained. Gradually the waves of their excitement subside and they float down into the normal state of being.

Ecstasy in art and music is perhaps more often reached than in the professions or in business, since art and music are emotionally tinged occupations. Vladimir A. is a highly capable conductor, although not very well known. He has worked with a number of small orchestras all over the world but, despite training in Russia and later in the United States, he has never reached the zenith of recognition. Nevertheless there are times during his work when he feels himself uplifted beyond the orchestra pit and transposed into a totally different state of being. Curiously, he has found this to be the case especially when conducting music by the composer Liszt. Liszt's music has often been called a fiery and emotionally stimulating experience. Somehow Vladimir and Liszt go together in a unique relationship. On one such occasion, and in the presence, fortunately, of a leading Paris critic, he gave what was surely his best performance conducting two major works by Franz Liszt. As a result, he received glowing reviews in the local papers. He was never able to repeat his performance, however, and has no knowledge of how it happened in the first place. Even when conducting the same pieces by Liszt the results are not the same.

Painters have sometimes created works that they were never able to explain themselves. Somehow a certain process within, unique and timed in a way that escapes detection, had come into operation at a given moment to allow them to

## Psycho-Ecstasy

create certain works of art. Fortunately the painter's work can be observed for long periods of time while the musician's work, especially if he is a conductor, can only be seen and heard at that very moment. Those artists who have experienced rare moments of ecstasy have described these states as being lifted from wherever they were standing as if their heads were reaching out into kind of a stratosphere. Their faces bathed by warm breezes they could not see, their ears ringing with strange whirring noises that were at once disturbing and exciting, their inner self experiencing both a total detachment from their surroundings and a state of timelessness in which they were not aware of anything but the force that surrounded them. Although these extraordinary states never lasted more than a few moments, to the one who experienced them they seemed to be eternities.

To reach the state of ecstasy deliberately as an artist is not an easy thing. It can be hoped for, it can be made a purpose in one's work, but it cannot be induced. Only by continually serving the purpose of one's art, in a true and pure sense, is one likely to experience such a state. It is necessary to identify completely with the nature of one's work, the character of one's book, the subject of one's painting, the message of one's music, anything that is created by the artist. It cannot be simply a piece of work created to be sold or exhibited; it must totally, in the deepest sense, represent the artist-creator. That is the first step. Then it is also necessary to accept the creation of one's work of art merely as a communication from a higher force to earth through the channel of oneself, the artist. The person who wishes to reach ecstasy in the arts can never consider himself as the *beginning* of his work. He is the receiver, not the giver. Ecstasy is his reward for having accomplished his task well and in the

## The Right-Hand Path

original spirit. He must carefully avoid any form of compromise, any form of pleasing others other than himself. Form is important in his training. It is of very little significance in the finished product if it is not a true expression of that which has motivated him to create it.

Ecstasy by the right-hand path is frequently difficult, strenuous and full of disappointment before one reaches the desired goal, if one reaches it at all. By the same token it is the only positive way to reach out towards that state unless one can apply certain helpful techniques to bring it about more assuredly and more quickly, techniques which I have explained in the next chapter of this book.

## Chapter IX

# PSE—Psycho-Ecstasy: A New Technique

The term PSE, meaning *psycho-ecstasy* is a term I have invented. For the purpose of this work, I should like to explain what psycho-ecstasy means to me, the first person to use this technical term.

Psycho, the first part of the word, refers to the fact that this particular ecstasy is reached through psychic means rather than by one of the other ordinary means described before. We are not going to deal in this chapter with ecstasy induced by artificial stimulation, by ordinary or natural efforts, or by any of the other means already known to man. This is a new technique different from any and all others previously discussed. The qualifying term, psycho, indicates that the state of ecstasy is reached through psychic induction. The term psychic itself should be defined here, also, as that which is derived from the extrasensory force within man. Being psychic means being able to have certain knowledge or abilities transcending the limits of the ordinary five senses as we currently understand them. The terms psychic, sensitive, medium are all interchangeable to a point. One need not be a professional or even an amateur medium in order to have psychic ability. A medium is someone actively using that ability in one way or another. Being psychic may be simply a latent state about which one does nothing. It is difficult to avoid having experiences, however, in the ordinary course of life. Thus, almost all those who are psychic will eventually have also mediumistic experiences in which their psychic ability comes into actual usage. In the ordinary sense, being psychic means that one is able to know about the future or about the past in a way that could not be obtained by ordinary means. Being psychic may also indicate the ability to have knowledge of events at a distance in space without recourse to orthodox sources of information.

But being psychic has a third, deeper meaning also—the ability to utilize more fully one's own inner force. There is in all of us, in addition to the physical and the mental, a third force—that of the spirit which has the unusual ability of seemingly contravening or altering the so-called natural laws of science. Those individuals who are more developed than the average person, in a spiritual sense, have psychic abilities. Their spiritual force is sufficiently strong to accomplish what to the uninstructed outsider seems like miracles. In effect, there are no such things as miracles in this universe. What is being accomplished through the application of psychic force is simply a fuller and more accurate utilization of powers which are latent in all of us but are recognized and fully used by a comparitively small number of people.

## Psycho-Ecstasy: A New Technique

What then are the peculiarities of the psychic force? I have already mentioned the ability to break into the future to see events that have not yet transpired, or to read the past of people one knows nothing about, or to gain knowledge, often instantaneously, of events at a distance with which one is not familiar or about which one is not informed in any way in the ordinary sense. That is how the term is generally understood.

When the psychic force is turned *inwardly*, however, the results are quite startling. By proper application of one's own psychic force one can overcome physical handicaps. For instance, one can suddenly find energy reservoirs one has not had a moment before and accomplish tasks that seem to be out of proportion to one's physical appearance or strength. In a general sense we are all familiar with the person who accomplishes a seeming miracle under great stress. A good case in point is that of Mrs. W. of Milwaukee, Wisconsin. Crossing the street one rainy day she was suddenly faced with a truck coming towards her at great speed. She was already in the clear, but her eleven-year-old son was right in the path of the onrushing truck. With "superhuman" speed she threw herself back into the roadbed, grabbed her son by the neck and pulled him to safety within a fraction of a second before the truck passed by. Normally, she is a frail, slow-moving woman. The sudden decision to act, the amazing jump she was able to make (back and forth) within such a short time period was entirely out of character in her case. Yet it came to pass under the pressure of sudden danger. It was not her physical self that accomplished this but a stronger inner force, a psychic force, that came into operation only when the danger signal had been flashed. Others have developed enormous physical endurance under great stress conditions.

One might argue that these sudden bursts of energy may

be connected with the life force and the desire to survive, and are essentially instinctively triggered. In some cases this is undoubtedly true, but in others no such reasoning or instinctive movement is involved.

On more than one occasion I have noticed that mediums in trance can develop amazing physical strength they do not possess in their everyday lives. Ethel Johnson Meyers is, by profession, a voice coach and her hands are gentle and frail. When she was entranced by the late financier, Serge Rubinstein, during the investigation of his murder in New York City, her hands gripped mine as if they were willing to break them to make me come with her to the place of the crime. For several days after I felt pain in the fingers she had so tightly held. Under ordinary conditions she would have never been able to apply such strength. On another occasion I saw these same hands push a heavy table clear across a room while under the influence of a discarnate entity bent on violence.

The important thing is, of course, to control this considerable amount of force within us and to apply it intelligently and where it will do some good. One must never forget that the same force is used constructively or destructively, depending upon the one directing it. When the psychic force is turned inwardly to accomplish goals, it is even more powerful then when it is sent forth from the one directing it. Inwardly the area of effect is more confined. The force is more concentrated and the need to be careful is even greater.

This force can be used to overcome any form of difficulty in reaching ecstasy, whether it be religious, professional, creative, or sexual ecstasy. First one must recognize what the physical or mental limitations are that one wishes to overcome. Where are the problems, the inhibitions, the diffi-

## Psycho-Ecstasy: A New Technique

culties? Most people are pretty certain as to what they would like to do and almost as certain why they can't accomplish it. If you can pinpoint the area of your weaknesses, you have already accomplished much of your goal. The psychic force is then directed to operate the body with all its reflexes, nerves and muscles to act contrary to ordinary limitations applying to you. This is done in the form of a gentle command coupled with the visualization of the accomplished desired result.

Father Bernard is now a well-liked, respected parish priest in the eastern United States. When he was still a young seminarian, he always despaired of becoming a priest and serving his community. The reason for this negative attitude was his inability to speak with conviction in a voice that would carry weight. Somehow he heard himself say things in his own head that didn't come out the same way when he had an audience. He knew that his voice was flat and that he often stammered, and he knew that what he had to say did not ring true to those listening to him. Yet he knew what to think and what he wanted to express, but somehow he was unable to bring it out into the open. Eventually, he became familiar with certain aspects of my technique. He directed his psychic force to apply itself, first of all, to his vocal cords to strengthen and relax them at the same time. He visualized this as happening several times during the week prior to an important sermon he was to deliver to his fellow students. Then he commanded the same psychic force to assure an uninterrupted flow of energy particles from his mind to his speech mechanism, that force not to be deflected in any way or to be interrupted by doubt, and to be forceful in his expression. This, too, he visualized several times. On the appointed day he delivered a flawless oration that earned him the highest praise possible. He has never since had problems exteriorizing his feelings and thoughts and has gone on to be a very successful preacher.

Louis J. loved selling things, many kinds of things, from vacuum cleaners to bedroom furniture. He is very successful in his difficult and tiresome profession, and he travels a great deal as is customary with this kind of work. Two years ago he decided to switch and concentrate on one product only. What he was going to sell would be far more important than anything he had ever sold before. He became a salesman for a new food additive which promised those taking it increased health and great physical awareness, as well as very little need for medical aid in the future. He had switched all his efforts to this one product because he had become convinced of its value himself and believed wholeheartedly that he would be doing a worthwhile thing if he were to sell this product to others. Thus the salesman turned into missionary for a cause.

He assumed that this would also convince others to buy his product, since he was now not merely selling a vacuum cleaner but something of great importance to humanity. Unfortunately, he found out otherwise. It wasn't that people refused to buy his product so much as his inability to bridge the gap between his good intentions and a believable sales presentation. The doors were open wide because he was a personable and charming man, but in a matter of a minute or two he had lost all the ground he might have gained by simply smiling. Somehow he could not put the right emphasis into his sales appeal. He became desperate and depressed, but not because he was losing money and not making sales. He had thought the product was a worthwhile product indeed and that he was contributing something other than merely his time and efforts to a commercial product.

## Psycho-Ecstasy: A New Technique

He meditated upon this for a while, having read some books on metaphysics. Somehow he found his way to the new techniques I am discussing here. He was taught to direct his psychic force to the center of his beliefs and to reinforce, first of all, his conviction that the food additive he was selling was not a fraud but an honest, worthwhile product. He fortified this psychic effort by reading everything he could on the subject of nutrition, only to find that he was right in the first place. Secondly, he directed his inner psychic force to give him the glow and sparkle of the believer so necessary to convince those he was to visit in order to sell the product. He went through several cycles of suggestion along the lines of psycho-ecstasy and developed a deep-seated fervor within himself that carried the message of his product into realms far beyond the commercial area. The following week he started out on a new route. Within two days he had sold all his product. Not only that, but people told their friends and before long he was invited as a speaker. The talent he had suddenly discovered within himself was, of course, due to his honest and strong conviction that he was doing the right thing at the right time with the right product. Within the same year he became a professional lecturer on the subject of nutrition, and the selling of the food additive that had started him in this direction became merely secondary. He began to "live" properly only when he was out in the field preaching his newly-found "gospel," sometimes reaching great heights of oratory, and letting a sincerity shine through his words which was communicated to those who listened to it.

Albert L. is a student at a northeastern university. When he was in high school he had been deeply in love with a classmate. They had found many things in common and had been close friends for several years. Slowly a feeling of love developed in her, too. It was Albert's complete conviction that they would eventually marry. Unfortunately, he was unable to sway his friend to such a degree that she would consent. They remained close friends, but their love relationship stagnated and led to great emotional turmoil in Albert, since he could not do anything about it and yet was unwilling and unable to break off the relationship. He tried various paths to solve his problem. Self-analysis, psychoanalysis, meditation—none of them really helped. They only strengthened his conviction that he was definitely meant for his friend Jane and she for him, but he was left wondering how he was to obtain this desire.

Eventually he became familiar with the techniques discussed here. He tried to awaken his inner psychic force by certain exercises, then directed it to help him in expressing his love feelings more accurately and more deeply to his intended bride. In the process, his character changed to a point where Jane wondered whether she was with a Jekyll and Hyde. Where he had been quiet and introverted ever since she had known him, he suddenly developed an outgoing personality, a flourish and a romantic inclination that he had never shown before. Though she was surprised, she accepted this change in Albert and assumed that it was part and parcel of growing up. As with many modern young people, they have had sexual relations all during their college years and at one time had lived together for a period of time, only to separate again when they discovered that their living together did not lead to a more permanent state of relationship. Three or four weeks after Albert had applied the psychic energy technique to himself, he decided to test his "new" personality and deliberately maneuvered Jane into going to bed with him. To her surprise she found herself vastly excited by his approach this time, and she wondered if the young man had secretly read some sex manuals. What was new to his approach to lovemaking, however, was not sexual technique. There was a deeper driving force to his approach to their union she had never known before. It seemed to her that Albert was "possessed" by some third force that eliminated his weakness, his shallowness and his hesitancy. None of this could be pinpointed in concrete terms, to be sure, but there was an overall feeling that Albert has become a different person. Not much later they decided to marry and they have lived together ever since.

These three examples are only a few from the dozens of cases in recent times where the successful application of the PSE or psycho-ecstatic principles has worked well and quickly. The height to which one may rise in any particular aspect, whether it is in the religious, professional, creative, the sexual and love aspect, depends entirely on the individual's ability to apply psychic force to reach the desired detachment from the earth-bound state of reality. There is nothing, in principle, to prevent anyone from reaching the highest levels of ecstasy when he or she follows these principles. The majority of people will probably want to apply them to more mundane or, shall we say, modest goals, finding the prospect of attaining them in itself rewarding. Those however who wish to reach out to the highest level of ecstasy can do so without danger and with the assurance that the proper application of the principles must yield the desired results.

What exactly are these techniques of PSE or psycho-ecstasy?

1. To begin the self treatment choose a quiet, semi-darkened room and close the windows partially. Let

in a little air but try to keep most of the noise outside. Pick a time of the day or night when you are reasonably sure to be undisturbed by either visits or telephone. A good time to start is when one is physically tired—at the end of the day, just before retiring, or immediately upon awakening before full consciousness has returned to the mind. But any other time is suitable as well, provided there is truly no interruption or distraction. Lie down on a couch or bed with your head slightly elevated and wear as little clothing as you can. The room should be neither too cold nor too warm, and it is always good to have a warm, relaxing bath prior to beginning the technique.

2. Speak in a slow, quiet voice the following phrase: "I _____ (insert your name), am myself and fully part of the godhead and part of the universe. I am with God and God is with me. Psychic force within me, arise!" Close your eyes now and visualize an energy flow within yourself originating from the solar plexus or stomach area and rising up towards the top of your head. Visualize it and feel it as a gentle stream of energy particles somewhat like a waterfall except that it goes in the opposite direction. Hold the thought of this phenomenon for a little while, increasing its strength gradually until it reaches the proportions of a powerful stream.

3. It is important to have a clean and clear mind free from all thoughts whether logical or emotional. If you have difficulties of cleansing your mind from interfering thought patterns, visualize yourself going

to a motion picture theater, sitting down in the dark auditorium and watching the very end of the motion picture pass before your eyes. When the final frames of the movie have passed, hold the idea of a blank silver screen before your eyes. This will empty your mind of all extraneous thoughts. You cannot have any form of emotional turmoil within you if you want this experiment to succeed. It is therefore important that, prior to beginning, you have already cleansed yourself of these interfering thought patterns. If you have difficulties in arousing this "stream of psychic power" within yourself go back to the beginning. Get up from the couch. Go through the entire ritual of preparing the room. If necessary, take a second warm bath and cleanse your mind again of all interfering thoughts. Then, start all over again. Eventually you will succeed in raising this power reservoir within you.

4. As you hold the visualization and thought of the psychic power within you as a stream, you order it to accomplish certain tasks upon which you have meditated beforehand. You then verbalize the command as follows: "Psychic energy within me, you are all-powerful. I direct you to make _____ do _____ (here the desired action is spelled out). You repeat this twice more in a slow, low, measured tone of voice.

5. After a minute or two of total rest in which you must be careful to avoid any extraneous thoughts whatsoever, you visualize the accomplished action as something that has already taken place. You see yourself

## Psycho-Ecstasy

with eyes closed having just done what you have already ordered your psychic force within to accomplish. You hold the idea and the picture of that accomplishment for as long as you can, then you speak again in the same tone of voice as you did before: "I\_\_\_\_\_ have done_____.My psychic power is omnipotent and omniscient. I am ecstatic. The power is mine. I am the power, so mote it be." This is followed by a few minutes of rest and some deep, measured breathing and then the exercise period is over.

These are the basic exercises forming the technique of PSE or psycho-ecstasy. How they apply in specific instances, and what some of the variations and more extreme possibilities are, we will discuss in the following chapters as we learn of the exact ways in which PSE or psycho-ecstasy can be applied—to help you get "out of yourself" into the higher realms of consciousness and derive all the benefits found therein.

## Chapter X
# Psycho-Ecstasy and the Religious Experience

A large segment of today's population, especially in the Western world, considers religion a department of their daily lives, something one must have, something one should practice and certainly admit to, but nothing to get all steamed up about. Religion to the average modern man no longer has the deeply emotional connotations it had originally in almost all civilizations and still has to a large segment of the population in certain areas. Religion, after all, means the link with the deity—a linking-up between mortal man and immortal God. This itself encompasses adventure of the highest kind. In this current age of materialism, whether of the capitalistic or the socialistic kind, the concept of a mystical involvement with an entity of higher power has gradually become obsolete in the thinking of man. There are even societies such as Soviet Russia where it is entirely unpopular, if not dangerous, to admit personal religious involvement.

Nevertheless there are millions of people who consider religion something more than a department of life in the manner of a job, insurance, car, home. For the religious individual the matter of his or her religious experience represents a major factor in his well-being, in his outlook towards a possible future life and in the way he deals with the other aspects of his daily life in the mundane sphere. The moral aspects of religion, as well as the theological aspects, may have great weight in the lives of individuals who are religiously oriented.

A much smaller segment of the world population goes beyond this personal involvement with religion. To them the religious experience supersedes the worldly life and must take precedence whenever there is any decision to be made. They view all developments in the world, whether personal or political, only from the religious point of view: How does it affect their beliefs? Is someone making decisions for the country that reflects their particular religious point of view? How would a certain action taken by them conflict with their religious convictions? They are the kind of people who view physical life merely as a temporary expression of the spiritual. Life in the hereafter is more important than life in the present.

Naturally those who make a career of their religion would be counted among such extremists. They are nuns, monks, priests, religious teachers, and philosophers whose central theme is the relationship between God and man. But even among laymen we have people who put their religious convictions ahead of everything else. Whenever their ordinary lives fail them they will seek refuge in their religion. Whenever a temptation arises in the form of some worldly pleasure beckoning to them, they will reject it on the grounds that it would take away energies from their religion. *In my view religious extremism of this kind is contrary to nature.* In the Christian religion and even in other faiths, we are reminded we must overcome nature or "the beast within." This is often misunderstood to mean that we must go against the natural laws. What is meant in the command to overcome nature or the beast within applies only to the baser instincts within us, not to *all* nature. God has created nature as His full expression. Man is part of that expression. Consequently man cannot possibly overcome something of which he forms a part, for in doing so he would go against the desire of the power that created him in the first place. The great schism between man and religion came about when man was commanded, by his religious leaders, to overcome all that is physical in nature and, by extension, in himself. Denying the life force both in the macrocosm and the microcosm inevitably leads to a parochial life alienated from nature, a life self-contained in the end. While it may conserve some of the energy within man in order to use it solely for intellectual processes, it also destroys the very base upon which all true religious experiences must be built, namely understanding of, and being in tune with Greater Nature.

Of the three groups of people named, the first and second are not likely to seek religious ecstasy consciously. It may occur in their lives spontaneously, unsought and to their surprise. Such was the case when a young girl experienced a spiritual vision in the cave of Lourdes. Such was the case whenever on the feast day of Saint Gennaio the blood of the saint liquified before the eyes of several thousand worshippers in a Naples church. Such may also be the case in a mass prayer meeting arranged by diverse political groups for the sake of the peace movement today. But only those for whom the religious experience represents the major factor in their lives will consciously hope for the point at which ecstasy is reached. Desiring this exalted state does not necessarily bring it about, of course. Many deeply devout persons have gone through their lives without ever experiencing anything remotely resembling a state of exaltation, despite the longing for it and despite their pious lives and despite prayers and full compliance with the laws and dogma of their respective faiths.

Psycho-ecstasy can be applied to the religious experience if that is what one wishes to do. It can serve first of all as a supplement to the ordinary way of reaching out to ecstasy, and by visualization and reinforcement of one's actions by psychic forces from within, it can give far greater emphasis to the actions one takes. Lip service to the religion belongs to the first group and frequently also to the second group discussed before. Personal involvement in religion generally applies to the third group, those for whom the religious experience represents the major factor in their lives. Personal involvement comes in many forms and at many levels. In the Christian religion we have the *Holy Roller* and similar, basically Baptist-oriented communities. In the Middle Ages there were two other groups of Christian followers dealing in personal involvement. They were called the *Flagellantes* because they would flagellate themselves to produce pain which, in turn, was to atone for the sins of the world and for their own sins. A second group called *Penitentes*, or sufferers, paraded through the streets, especially in Latin countries, in monks' habits and hoods, giving the impression of total

## PSE and Religious Experience

anonymity. Even today there are sporadic displays of this kind of religious involvement, especially in certain Latin American countries.

Among Jews, there are sects such as the Chasidims whose personal involvement forces them to exhaust themselves in strenuous dancing and chanting. A similar approach to "getting out of themselves" religiously is practiced by the whirling dervishes of Iran and the Near East. And in West Africa, voodoo, which is also practiced in Haiti and many other parts of the Caribbean and southern United States, uses exhausting dance rituals coupled with vocal outcries to approach a similar state. The physical movement is intended to exhaust the body to a point where the tie between conscious and unconscious is lessened and the true self can rise above its physical limitations to seek out the plane of ecstasy.

Any person planning to participate in one of the above-mentioned rites, who is fully aware of the implications, but not sure of success, can insure reaching that state by using psycho-ecstatic techniques prior to engaging in the religious practices.

In a quiet moment before joining the religious community practicing these rites, one will visualize one's own participation in them and command the psychic force to rise in the manner already described. Once this is felt within, the specific command is given that this force shall be present during the religious ceremony one is to attend, and to lift oneself into the realm of the ecstatic. It is important to formulate these verbal commands in as brief and concise a manner as possible. Phrases such as: "I command thee psychic force within me to assist me in raising myself above the physical level into ecstasy; I command thee psychic force within me to overcome all hindrances and obstacles and to assure that I

## Psycho-Ecstasy

shall not fail in my attempt to reach ecstasy," will be found most useful, and if properly applied with the right conviction and intonation, they will be effective for the individual.

A less strenuous approach to the religious experience involves a combination of prayer and promise. In ancient times this was accomplished by a sacrifice of sorts, not necessarily a living sacrifice, but either the gift of something valuable or the promise to give up something which one ordinarily would want to do or possess. Sacrifice therefore involves either putting an object upon the altar or depriving oneself of something desirable. The idea behind sacrifices is that in giving up one thing one is eligible for another. It is a very primitive approach to the deity, of course, since it assumes that the deity has need of sacrifice. Strange as it may seem, the oldest of all religions, Wicca or White Witchcraft, does not believe in sacrifice at all. "The oldest religion" already knows that the deity cannot be bought, bribed or otherwise influenced to make just decisions. But even the most sophisticated of Christian churches still include rituals involving sacrifice. Whether it is merely the purchase of a candle in honor of the Mother of God or a specific saint, or a promise not to eat meat for a certain period of time, or to come to mass regularly when one has not done so for some time, some form of promise is involved. In earlier times wealthy people would promise to build a chapel or church in honor of a particular saint in payment for special favors asked of the deity.

The prayer, coupled with the promise and some form of gift, is, however, grounded not so much in a conviction that the deity will smile upon one because of it, as upon a very human trait of wanting to receive full value for one's offering. This is entirely selfish and man-conceived, of course,

## PSE and Religious Experience

since we have no proof that the deity demands anything in payment which will produce the desired results.

The techniques of psycho-ecstasy may at least create a higher state of anticipation in such cases. Once the psychic force within is raised in the usual manner, the command is given to perform the offering, the sacrifice, the promise as fully as possible. In addition, the inficidual will assure himself that he has done something specific to earn the desired reward. The conviction of having done so properly and successfully is reinforced through the rising power and projected as something that has already taken place, even if it has not. The exaltation of having sacrificed is then translated into a state of ecstasy because one feels freed from the weight of performing the sacrifice. It is already a matter of record, one has earned one's reward, and the psychic force drives one up into the higher levels of consciousness where one may justly enjoy a state of bliss.

I have already mentioned White Witchcraft or Wicca, the religion of the Stone Age, which has continued to exist, even though underground, until this day. One of the prime elements sustaining Wicca is the use of sympathetic magic to obtain results. In sympathetic magic the practitioner indicates something he wants to happen. For instance, if a good hunt is desired, the witchcraft priest will don the skin of a dead animal and prance around in the forest. This is not done to attract other animals who wouldn't possibly be fooled by it, but to create an *atmosphere* in which other animals may also be hunted and slain. If a higher crop is desired the witch will jump as high as he or she can to indicate how high the crop should grow. It doesn't pull the seed out of the soil, but it creates again an atmosphere in which the crop may indeed follow the suggestion of sympathetic magic. This jumping, by

## Psycho-Ecstasy

the way, is done astride a broomstick or staff. The broomstick is the ancient symbol of domesticity. The ritual of showing the crop how high to grow has been misunderstood, and in later centuries witches were accused of riding through the sky on broomsticks, which they decidedly did not do. If there is today a witch wanting to perform sympathetic magic of one or the other kind, he or she would find the results greatly strengthened by the use of psycho-ecstasy techniques. Although it would not create a state of personal ecstasy, it would make the ritual deeper and more meaningful and as a result more effective.

Both Eastern and Western religions acknowledge individuals practicing asceticism. An ascetic denies the physical world, the self, the demands of nature, the pleasures of the world and all that which constitutes nature's greatest gift. Instead, the ascetic prefers self-denial, isolation and long periods of meditation. With the deprivation of food and drink and the suppression of bodily functions as much as possible, the energies within are directed towards a more intellectual goal. This too results in the loosening of bonds between the physical and the spiritual, and may open a gateway to the godhead. Ascetics frequently report seeing God or Jesus Christ or other spiritual leaders of their religion in person. They are capable of having visions of being "transported" spiritually long distances, developing psychic abilities in general and becoming, in the popular view, holy men. In some cases the ascetic road leads to the gift of healing. In others the laying-on of hands is replaced by the ability to walk over fire or hot coals without burning one's skin. The Indian Fakir is the mundane expression of a similar principle. The Tibetan yogi accomplishes many feats of seeming miracles including total control of bodily functions.

## PSE and Religious Experience

What is the purpose of overcoming the body, the physical, the joys of the world? In the Western traditions it is to be in the presence of God, to partake of the spiritual experience, to be among His saints while still in the flesh. In the Eastern traditions it indicates a blending into nirvana, the state of total bliss where individuality gradually ceases. In orthodox Judaism the desired state is one of total understanding of the scriptures to the point where not only every word has deeper and manifold meanings but even individual letters carry deeply religious significance, inner meanings, the answers to puzzles the ordinary man cannot ever understand. Thus among Hebrew scholars there is a preoccupation with the meaning of words rather than with the implications of the scriptures. In a somewhat different way the modern Baptist emphasizes the literalness of the Holy Bible.

In all these instances physical denial has already opened a wedge towards ecstasy. Those who are of this bent may induce it for sure by having the raising of the psychic force within do it. First, the command is given to strengthen their ability to continue to deny themselves the pleasures of this world. Commands such as "I shall not crave food. I shall not crave physical pleasures or lust," will be sufficient to create a heightened state of rejection of the so-called temptation. On a positive level the command will be "I shall be with the Lord and understand Him," or similar phrases of direction indicating the desired results. Together with the practices here described, the result in many cases will be one of ecstasy in which the personal, direct religious involvement with the deity is complete. For those who seek it, it represents complete fulfillment of life. To themselves, such people are above all ordinary individuals, and nothing going on in the mundane world can ever affect or hurt them. In a manner of speaking

## Psycho-Ecstasy

they are happy, but religious ecstasy, no matter how well intentioned, has one fatal flaw. There is no indication that the deity demands it of us, nor is there any reason why the deity should need it for its own increase. The deity, after all, is complete unto itself. Thus religious ecstasy, as any other ecstatic state, ultimately represents merely just one facet of man's desire to fulfill himself for his *own* reasons and ends.

## Chapter XI
# Psycho-Ecstasy and the Creative Expression

Two people may do the same work or create similar art objects, yet one will find general acceptance, even universal praise, while the other merely satisfies a small number of requirements and "gets by." Yet, inherently, both are equally talented, equally honest, and try about as hard as they are able to. The difference lies in the something extra one of the two puts into the effort. That something extra, in the few cases where universal acceptance is the result of the effort, is sometimes referred to as genius, sometimes as talent, and at other times as plain good luck. All three descriptions make it a decidedly rare occurence and remove it from the control of the individual. In using the techniques of PSE, psycho-ecstasy, however, we attempt to improve certain aspects of

## Psycho-Ecstasy

one's personality or effort to the point where they reach beyond the commonplace. In the case of creative expression, it means that we can change a good piece of work into a brilliant, significant effort. The difference between average results and extraordinary accomplishment lies in the proper application of these techniques. Whatever the work may be, whether it is in the world of business and involves commercial accomplishments, or whether it is in the arts and revolves around performance, creation of art objects, or what have you, essentially we are dealing with an expression of human productivity in the material sphere. Even an artist must reconcile himself to the materialistic aspects of the world in which he works. His creation may be of a spiritual or intellectual nature, but the marketplace in which he sells it or the world in which he finds recognition is a material world. Consequently, he must reckon with the values that material world will put on his services and accomplishments. Professional accomplishment therefore inevitably involves a material aspect. The reception accorded to an intellectual or artistic victory may be honor, praise, or recognition, but in an indirect way these verbal reactions by the world or the public lead to material expressions of success. No matter how intangible the acknowledgement is it represents the opening wedge to many tangible results and may well change the habit and outlook of the one receiving it.

There is no exception to this rule. The public speaker or politician whose points are well taken, who knows his facts and presents them well, may be just one of many who are competent, acceptable, intelligent and well liked. But, unless something extra enters his speech making, he will not emerge the leader, he will not become a symbolic expression only of the idea for which he stands. There are many teachers whose

## PSE and Creative Expression

training has prepared them well for their jobs. They teach with competence and confidence and in a proper manner, yet among them there will be a few sought out by students because of an extra quality—the way they present the same facts that thousands of others present without being able to inject that "something extra." Philosophies have been stated and restated later in almost the same way, yet at first hearing they did not convince anyone, while the *new* version did.

Something has been added, not so much in the choice of words but in the way these words were put before the public. Two researchers may be armed with the same blueprint and may wind up with totally different results. One man following simply that which he was trained to do will come up with expected results, while the other, driven by an unseen force that is still hard to define accurately, will turn in new directions at certain points in his research, and because of this move, come up with unexpected, startling results of great significance in his work.

Medical doctors may be familiar with all the latest knowledge of the profession, yet a few among them will have extraordinary success with patients for reasons one cannot accurately define. The few outstanding healers simply have a certain touch which enables them to pinpoint the malady of the patient more accurately, perhaps sooner, perhaps also finding a remedy for it from among many remedies possible and succeeding where others in their profession have failed. Yet, if we tried to analyze the reasons why a few outstanding individuals succeed more readily than others in their professions, we will come up to a blank wall. The reasons cannot be analyzed, they cannot be put into so many words. There is only one thing all these outstanding individuals have in common in addition to their training, to their knowledge, to their proper qualifications. They have some extra factor in their personalities that enables them to make the right decisions, to say the right thing at the proper time, or to act in such a way that their words are more convincing than the words of others, even the same words in someone else's mouth.

What then is the extra factor that seems to be decisive in lifting the results from the commonplace into the extraordinary? Quite clearly it is not further learning, further information or greater skill in handling the information one already possesses. It is not judgment in case of doubt, it is not greater physical force, greater application of mental force or anything that could be defined as easily as that. It is, however, an *attitude*. It is the inner attitude of one's own personality directed towards the subject of one's efforts that influences the results. This attitude differs from the ordinary attitude of competence in that it involves a sense of enthusiasm for the work at hand, an inner excitement expressed through psychic vibrations that permeate the entire body and mind in such a way that a state of altered consciousness is reached. In this state, ordinary action, words, expressions take on a different dimension. The difference between this state and the ordinary state corresponds roughly to the difference between black and white photographs and full color pictures. Something has been added, yet the basic situation is still there. It merely looks different because of the extra factor. The involvement of the inner self at the psychic level makes the difference.

Now you can't command this at will nor can you coldly plan it or study for it. This state of ecstasy can, however, be reached by certain techniques, provided one is convinced that it is a desirable condition to be in. This is not as unimportant as it may sound at first. The conviction is very necessary.

## PSE and Creative Expression

When the desire for a state of psycho-ecstasy becomes a routine intent, it may very well not work any longer. Make it desirable only when you are convinced that important issues are at stake. These may not be of world-shaking significance but important to you as an individual. Psycho-ecstasy should never be invoked when other methods may yield similar or adequate results. Do not waste it on situations not worthy of the effort, but if you are convinced that only the state of psycho-ecstasy can bring you the desired results then be assured that you can reach this state through the techniques mentioned here.

Frank G. lived a very difficult life as a so-called Greenwich Village poet, practically starving and subsisting on occasional odd jobs which he hated. His poetry was neither very good nor very bad, but it was quite professional, for Frank had gone to school and wrote good English. But it didn't get published very often and when it was published it didn't sell. Frank despaired. He was ready to forsake all efforts to become a writer and turn to other pursuits. Through a friend he learned of techniques described in this work. Drawing upon his inner psychic power, he visualized himself saying what he wanted to say in a grander, more eloquent manner than he had been able to before.

To be sure, he did not hear the exact words, he merely experienced the feeling of being tremendously successful in expressing himself, and he added the visualization of acceptance by the great masses of people he wanted to reach. He went through these exercises daily at the same time. Gradually he increased the amount of poetic visions transmitted in this manner and elaborated more and more on the reaction of his listeners. He would do this with his eyes closed sometimes for half an hour, sometimes for a full hour. His body was

## Psycho-Ecstasy

relaxed since he did his exercises lying down. After three or four weeks of this he noticed a change in his style. His phrases flowed more easily, more freely, and he discovered a joyful expression in his work which he had lacked before. While he had labored to bring forth the most nearly perfect, the most expressive sentence up to then, he now found that it all came to him much easier, that he didn't have to think it out first, that he merely had to put on paper what had come to him seemingly from an outside source. He realized, of course, that *the source* was not really outside of himself but that it had merely inspired his inner self to let go of its powers more freely. Gradually his poetry became better and better and he found a new publisher. Within a matter of two months after publication of his latest volume of poetry, some of his poems were set to music and a record album made. Frank was well on his way to success and to the joy of knowing that his work was truly appreciated by a great number of people. Because he is so well known I have not given his true name here, but I've seen him recently and he seemed to me like a new man.

Let us say you are a sculptor or a painter. You are insecure about the success of your work, you know you are good, you know you have learned all the professional techniques and you are not an amateur. Psycho-ecstasy does not replace learning and routine training, but it can sometimes raise a good professional into a genius. You decide that a certain work of art will be your masterpiece, and that in creating it you will test your success with the critics and with the public at large. How can you assure this success?

First, convince yourself that this is your chance to make it in a big way. Convince yourself that you have the ability and that you want to succeed and come to public attention, and

## PSE and Creative Expression

that this will be the time when it will happen. Build within yourself this firm inner conviction that the time is at hand to make a big name for yourself. This may take you a few days but eventually it will sink into your unconscious that the time for the big attempt has come.

Then start the exercises. As you work on the artistic project you have in mind, keep visualizing its completion. For the first week visualize only the completion of the work of art, what it will look like, what it will feel like and how you feel about it at that moment. Do not go further than that. Lie down in a comfortable place for half an hour every day. Visualize your masterpiece as it grows from the beginnings to the end. When you have held the vision of its completion, let your whole body be filled with a sense of warmth and pride because you have accomplished what you have set out to do. The second week add to this visualization. Visualize now the reception of your work and yourself by the critics. Visualize newspaper headlines proclaiming it as a major work of art. Create in your mind conversations about it. After a few days of this exercise, add impressions of the general public to the reception afforded you by the critics. Invent imaginary conversations between passersby discussing your work of art. Visualize even foreigners talking about it. Whatever your imagination allows you to create in your own mind, let it have free rein. After two weeks of this you are ready to raise the power within. As you approach the actual completion of your work, the time is at hand to send forth the thought form to those who can actually judge your work and thus create the new you which you have desired for yourself.

It is important to time this very carefully. Do not attempt this final set of exercises until the work is actually ready to be unveiled. If you need additional time, keep up the other exercises of visualization, adding various touches here and there or repeating former visualizations. When the work of art is finished and ready to be presented to the public and the critics, begin a series of exercises in which you raise the psychic power. You draw it from the solar plexus in the stomach area slowly towards the second solar plexus at the top of your head. With your eyes closed you visualize and suggest the increase of this power until it reaches its greatest strength. At this point you release it suddenly, commanding it to go forth and create ecstatic responses in those viewing your work of art. Do this for a number of days prior to the opening or the unveiling of the specific work of art you are trying to elevate above the commonplace. On the eve of the day do it for the last time. On the day itself put yourself in a state of complete repose and make your mind as much a blank as possible. The work is done. Let the power make itself felt.

If you are a performing artist such as an actor or a singer, much of your work lies in the way you appear to the critics or audience. Therefore the psycho-ecstasy must be within your person. You may start in the same way as with the creative artist, who works with tools, canvas or stone, by suggesting critical and audience reaction to your work. Visualize your performance and any and all details you can conjure up from your imagination. After you have reached a point when the performance is due, on the eve of it draw the power within from the lower solar plexus to the upper solar plexus and release it by sudden command. Command it to go out on the appointed day and surround yourself as well as the audience with a sense of ecstasy. It is important to visualize yourself as filled with the *same* psycho-ecstasy, at

## PSE and Creative Expression

the time you are "reaching out" to touch the emotional stimulation centers of your audience. As a final move, visualize yourself as raised above the ground quite literally, performing the well-rehearsed play or musical composition in the manner that will transport your audience to a point where they will share your ecstatic feelings. With the sculptor and painter it is not necessary for the artist to be included in the psycho-ecstasy created by their work of art, but with the performer this is absolutely necessary. If you are a writer then the technique applying to sculptor and painter would also be appropriate for you, except that the visualization centers on the appearance of the book and on the message of it rather than on the appearance of the work of art alone as with sculptor and painter. You may add to this the auditory elements of repeating certain key paragraphs of your work and visualizing a particularly favorable reception to those passages by critics or audience. You may even invent critical quotes that you would like to hear or see in print praising your book or article or play.

The same approach may be used in every form of expression, whether it is in a creative field such as the arts or in a commercial field such as business or the professions. One can always find certain key factors, certain key scenes or verbalizations representing success in one's chosen work. The visualization and commands concentrate on these particular aspects of one's work. It is, of course, very important to channel one's efforts directly. Don't be vague in expressing your desires. The tighter one is able to marshal one's thoughts in expressing the *exact* results desired, the more likely the results will be favorable. Psycho-ecstasy, PSE, does not do the thinking for you. You yourself have to come to terms with your desires. Psycho-ecstasy technique merely

## Psycho-Ecstasy

shows you how to turn a desire into an accomplishment. Expressing one's desires simply and in as few words as possible is not the easiest thing in the world. It has been said that it isn't so difficult to get what you want. What is difficult is to know what you want. Psycho-ecstasy does not tell you what to want, it tells you how to get it once you know it. Only your own judgment can tell you what you wish to accomplish. Your inner convictions that you are on the right track in desiring such and such, even though you may not be convinced that you can obtain favorable results, are therefore of paramount importance, as I have already pointed out.

Assuming that you know what you want and that you work the exercises well, success will be yours. As a result, new confidence is instilled in you and your next effort may not even require these techniques to succeed. Anything you have done once you may do again. This is not conjecture but a law of nature. If you have accomplished it with your own resources then you may use them a second time. Keep in mind that the use of psycho-ecstasy techniques does in no way take away from your own inner resources or talents. Without them, psycho-ecstasy would not have succeeded. The techniques described here enhance your inherent qualities. They do not create them or in any way replace them. You therefore need not think that the use of these techniques is a crutch or subterfuge. You are neither cheating nor competing unfairly, you are merely using all that is available to you which, unfortunately, many people are not aware of. It is expanded knowledge of your inner powers that makes you successful, not a miracle, not external powers nor anything your competitor may not also have access to, if he so desires.

## PSE and Creative Expression

What exactly happens when the power raised within you is sent forth to influence or impress critic or public or, as in the case of the performer, permeate you also to give a different kind of reading or rendition? Here is what happens: The positive image accomplished, which you have "broadcast" a number of times prior to the actual happening of the event, becomes superimposed onto the objective happening itself. It creates an extra layer the way a doubly printed image might on photographic film. This extra layer creates extra depth, an extra dimension, and, of course, extra excitement. You are doing what you would normally do except a little more of it. More of your "essence" reaches the sensory organs of the audience, and stimulates them to a larger degree than the ordinary three-dimensional reality would. Thus the audience stimulation reaches up into the ecstatic. Your pre-recorded broadcast, to use a conventional television term, becomes fused with the live broadcast of whatever it is you wish to impress the audience with. You have added extra guns to your fortifications. The difference between the normal level of consciousness and the ecstatic level is that extra push which you are able to give your brainchild through the techniques and exercises described here. They are, in a sense, exteriorized wish fulfillment.

Since all thought forms are electrical impulses traveling at great speed and containing tiny particles of electromagnetic substance imprinted with part of your emotions, these thought forms reach out to the sensory organs of other human beings and convey the desired thought to them. They, that is the audiences, respond automatically, as it were, since the thought image has reached them at the emotional, unconscious level. They cannot help but respond favorably

## Psycho-Ecstasy

since no logical sifting of the material takes place within them. You are getting to them at the level where the response is instantaneous and direct.

It is clear that these techniques could be of tremendous value in the political arena. We in this country have not used them in any sense to influence the masses. Soviet Russian scientists are well aware of the implications of telepathy and have hurriedly started to study ESP in all its facets. Billions have been poured into research in recent years. In America there is no money of significance available in these areas of research. So far, no major politician has come forward using the techniques of PSE or psycho-ecstasy. Tomorrow, there may be such a man. Picture, if you will, the implications of concisely expressing political slogans prior to a mass meeting or perhaps prior to a television lecture. While the techniques do not work as well through television or radio, since the immediacy of a live audience is absent, they will work to a certain degree even by remote control or on film, since we are dealing here with electromagnetic particles which are adequately represented by the image on the home screen or the radio speaker. The strongest appeal, however, a politician might find by using psycho-ecstasy techniques would involve a live audience in a closed area such as a large hall. It should be remembered that psycho-ecstasy techniques can be applied both positively and negatively. They do not carry any moral convictions and are available to anyone whether of good will or otherwise.

Since a politician is, in a manner of speaking, also a performer, part of his raised power will enter his own personality and imbue him with a sense of the ecstatic. This represents great potential dangers, since in some instances it may create the illusion, in the politician, of being a divinely chosen leader.

## PSE and Creative Expression

While the techniques mentioned here have not been in existence, as such, for very long, parallel approaches have at times been made in widely scattered areas of the world. Even Adolf Hitler used his evil genius in a similar way to elicit emotional responses from his mass audiences. Here then is the danger of psycho-ecstasy techniques when dealing with political objectives. If the individual employing the techniques is not free from egomania, he may mistake the power raised *by himself* through inner concentration as something put upon him by outside forces. In our times this may manifest itself as a sense of destiny; in earlier times it may have been called the hand of God. But if used improperly such power can be abused into forcing an audience to follow blindly, whether or not the objectives of the leader are moral and proper.

True psycho-ecstasy results in a sense of enthusiasm, always on the positive side, that leaves the audience with a feeling of joyful fulfillment. There can never be any sense of destruction or hatred for others resulting from the experience of psycho-ecstasy. Beware of such tendencies if they should ever occur in your life. If an evil movement were to be counteracted by these techniques, it would not be through destruction of the movement but through the upgrading of it by the injection of new, positive elements into that movement, rather than by colliding with it head on. A psycho-ecstatic person elevates himself above the level of the commonplace. Consequently, he can afford to be compassionate under all circumstances.

It is useless and detrimental to question the validity of these techniques once one has come to the conclusion that one wants to employ them. One should no longer doubt their efficiency. The expression of any doubt, no matter under what guise, is tantamount to poor application of the techniques. Critical or analytical observation of the techniques while one employs them is equally useless. We are dealing here with emotional immersion, and anything but a wholehearted approach will fail. When you use psycho-ecstasy to improve your creative expression or your work, whatever it may be, you must leave your ordinary, everyday approach to it behind. You cannot apply the old standards and at the same time learn the new ones. A confident attitude which is both hopeful and positive, and yet not blindly demanding, is best when pursuing the techniques.

It should be remembered also that psycho-ecstasy techniques are not absolutes and that their application and the result differs greatly from individual to individual. This is as it should be, since they are extensions of individual personality and by no means a rigid external system equally applicable to one and all.

It may seem strange to suggest such techniques in scientific research, but they are as applicable here as they are in the more emotionally motivated arts and crafts. In research there are moments when a scientist is literally "up the creek," when he does not know which way to turn next. He may grope for an answer which escapes him. He may have come to a point where there are several possibilities and where he is not sure which way to turn next, or he may be looking for a link somewhere in the vast realm of science and does not know where to look first. It may take him years, perhaps a lifetime, to locate the next step by logical or ordinary means. It is at such a juncture of events that the psycho-ecstasy techniques may turn frustration or a stalemate into success. The scientist cannot visualize performance the way an actor or singer does, or critical acclaim of his work of art as painter and sculptor does. He, in turn, must visualize the ultimate

## PSE and Creative Expression

success of his research, the final step in his particular endeavor, without being able to visualize even the intermediary steps leading towards it. If he can do this, sharply defined and without questioning, he will then obtain the intermediary steps also through visualization, in that flashes of consciousness will emerge during the exercise and link up with the final, visualized results. He is, of course, drawing upon powers within him and upon knowledge he is not aware of but possesses nevertheless. This is not searching out by extrasensory means information from the beyond, or looking for spiritual help, but the opening of deep levels of consciousness within which would not yield to ordinary search. By visualizing the desired results and the ecstatic reception by the scientific community of these findings, a scientist is, in fact, creating the conditions that will allow him to find the intermediary links.

In a similar way, a medical man may proceed if he has the courage to employ the techniques of psycho-ecstasy. Where his medical textbooks fail him the techniques may well supply the answer. This is especially important, since a medical man deals with the human personality as a whole, not with a machine. By visualizing the fully healed patient he may very well create a sense of ecstasy both for the patient and for himself: for the patient by sending forth the accomplished state of health and for himself by setting up the visualization of the steps he is to take to help his patient become well. In this case, however, it is important to exclude all critical thought or references to textbooks if these textbooks have not yielded significant clues to the accomplished or desired feeling.

When PSE, psycho-ecstasy techniques, are applied to one's work, the results are the main criteria of accomplishment.

They are, of course, the surest way of knowing whether or not one has succeeded, but one should not overlook a secondary aspect. Having used the psycho-ecstasy techniques successfully gives one not only the very real success for which one has been working but an inner sense of accomplishment which was not present prior to entering on the course described here. The very fact that psycho-ecstasy techniques are being used also changes one's inner self.

Where prior to the attempt one may have been hesitant about one's own powers, the constant usage of these powers creates a deeper sense of involvement with self. Better knowledge of one's own abilities in this respect results. It may well be that with future attempts to reach psycho-ecstatic levels, fewer exercises will be necessary. A readier and quicker response will be forthcoming if exercises are continued over long periods of time. However, this must not become a routine and should not be done without purpose or cause. Finally, one should not be surprised if ordinary people who are not familiar with psycho-ecstatic techniques will take a new look at the person who has been using these techniques. Somehow you will appear to be different, more radiant, more confident. You may be hard put to explain what has happened to you. Even your physical appearance may undergo changes, since the minute electromagnetic particles set in motion within you also create beneficial disturbances in the molecular structure of the body. You may, in fact, become more attuned to nature, more in balance with your world, and a certain undefinable but very real glow of health will surround you. PSE, psycho-ecstasy, is not merely a visualization of thought forms but a very real revolutionary process involving all aspects and levels of your personality.

## Chapter XII
# Psycho-Ecstasy and the Union of the Sexes

It appears that the 1970s are trying to make up for the lack of sexual manuals of the Victorian Age. What was sadly wanting in the nineteenth century seems to be available in abundance. So much so, in fact, that it is difficult to differentiate between the genuinely informative and the merely prurient. Books on sexual intercourse are freely displayed in book stores, even advertised in such media as the *New York Times*. There are essentially two kinds of works dealing with presumably improved sexual relations: those written by medical men and informed laymen dealing in a sincere and direct way with the various problems existing between partners of the opposite sexes, and those written by professional writers intent on exploiting the general interest and greater

## Psycho-Ecstasy

freedom of discussion nowadays possible on the subject of sex.

Clearly the subject is not new. From the beginning of time man had an interest in a member of the opposite sex, and it was never considered taboo to discuss this subject, that is, the question of sexual relations, *in private*. Where times and cultures differ widely is in the explicitness with which the subject can be discussed in public or in print.

The subject of sexual gratification has always been closely related to the religious experience. In the Stone Age religion sex formed an integral part of the ritual at certain times, as in the marriage act or in certain rare and highly advanced fertility rites. It was never totally absent but no undue stress was put upon it either. All primitive religions, East or West, have considered the creative urge in man as sacred. The sexual organs have always been venerated in this connection not for what we would call today lewd reasons, but, to the contrary, for very sacred and solemn reasons. The miracle of birth has endowed the female sexual organs with the aura of mystery. The male organ, the phallus, as the initiator of the creative process has always been venerated as such. The wonder of woman nursing her child and the fact that mother milk is a perfect food has caused woman's breasts to be represented in religious ceremonies from the very earliest times on. As these societies became more sophisticated, symbolic representations of the organs took the place of the rudimentary, basic forms.

To this day man doesn't completely understand the process of procreation in himself and in nature. If he understands it to a large degree, he understands the mechanics but he certainly does not know who instituted the laws that govern them. On minute analysis it becomes evident that

## PSE and Union of the Sexes

everything is well-arranged and nothing is either superfluous or ill-fitting in the process of procreation. But sexual intercourse is not merely an instrument for the continuance of the human race. It is clearly primarily a process whereby the two polarities among human beings join forces for a third purpose, that of achieving a greater entity than their own component parts.

It is a sad comment upon our times to say that not too many people achieve this greater entity from within themselves. After long periods of suppression in the Western world, the question of a better sexual union has come to the surface where it can be freely analyzed and discussed. In the East, especially in India, it has always been a subject accepted matter-of-factly, but never on the *outside*. Inside his house the Easterner is free to indulge in unusual sexual practices. He wouldn't dream of putting a display of nudity upon the public stage or market square. The Westerner on the other hand frequently admires such displays when they are public while he would not engage in unusual practices in his own home.

The institution of marriage, which has existed from the beginning of time also, clearly necessitates the existence of a third factor in the sexual relationship between the partners if that relationship is to continue for long periods of time. Continuous fresh stimulation is a contributing factor to potent sexual arousal. This is similar to the belief in the Eastern mystery religions that the surprise element is vital to a deep religious experience. Familiarity does not breed contempt in either sex or religion but it lessens the interest and ability to concentrate. This is not deliberate but merely a fact of life. If the surprise element of continually changing partners is removed from sexual union other elements must take its place.

## Psycho-Ecstasy

There are three basic forms in which men and women practice sexual union. There is, first of all, the basic animalistic approach requiring no preparation, no foreplay, no spiritual-mental stimulation of any kind. The only instinct satisfied is the instinct of the nervous impulses involved. The organs, through mechanical action, go through their proper natural involvement. When the act itself is completed there is no residue, no continuance, nor is there any desire to see in the act itself any more than purely physical relief. At this low level the sexual union is little more than a discharge of built-up tensions. If a marriage contract is built upon that kind of approach it cannot possibly last very long since familiarity of the partners must eventually weaken the results.

Secondarily, there is the great bulk of people practicing sexual intercourse on a dual level. If they are marriage partners they will express their love and desire for each other through the physical act. They will enhance the feelings of the mechanical interplay between their bodies by self-suggestion and visualizations in which the idea of the marriage bond predominates. Because one loves the other partner one ought to experience joy from this physical union. Sometimes it is because one enjoys the physical union that one ought to love one's marriage partner. Whether it works in one direction or the other way does not matter, so long as both reasons are simultaneously expressed. When familiarity blunts the edges of excitement in these unions, the emotional impact of continued partnership will carry them through additional years until, eventually, a purely emotional relationship alone will suffice for the validity of the marriage. This kind of relationship has the best chance to be deepened and broadened by mutual consent, by a better knowledge of the physical apparatus, and by frequent discussions of the meaning of the act itself as time goes on. It requires, however, that the two partners are in tune with each other, that they share many mutual interests, and above all are joined in the same or similar philosophical beliefs. There is no question that the result of sexual union can suffer greatly when there are continuing tensions between the partners. These tensions need not be physical but may be emotional or even spiritual. They must first be lowered or eliminated altogether if the union is to take place with a reasonable expectancy of fulfillment.

The third type of sexual union found generally among people balances the elements strongly in favor of the spiritual-emotional aspect of the partnership. Here the sexual union is merely a token expression of their coming together, undertaken at infrequent intervals, and, in a sense, it seems distasteful by comparison with the high spiritual level of their otherwise "unblemished" relationship. Very imaginative people sometimes have this kind of relationship. Their sexual union produces the children, and there is an occasional coming together for the sake of old memories or because the other partner feels it is time to have sex once again. But the bulk of their relationship is found in their spiritual unity, in their sharing of ideas rather than deeds. Such marriages can outlast those built upon physical attraction and can fulfill the partners in exactly the same way a more balanced union would. This requires, however, that both partners be very much alike in their demands and in their needs for physical fulfillment.

People no longer suppress their problems when it comes to sexual maladjustment. In former years one had a tendency to disregard such problems when they existed, and women especially were more prone to accept the subordinate role in the sexual partnership. Today they demand an equal share, and if there are difficulties between partners, consultations with psychologists or psychiatrists take place to remedy the situations. A more aggressive outlook on the part of the female in sex relationships has made it possible to discuss some delicate aspects of these unions without fear of embarrassing anyone.

It is therefore not for the purpose of shocking my readers or to dwell on unsavory details that I am suggesting that PSE, psycho-ecstasy techniques, may be applied for the greatest degree of fulfillment any two people can derive from their union. It is important that the sexual union be as perfect as possible *for as long* as possible, in fact, for their entire lives. So much depends on this aspect of intimate relationships that any effort to improve these relationships will have repercussions on other levels as well. The mundane world of expression, the world of personal and professional success, the state of health, even the state of one's spiritual self are all involved in varying degrees and cannot be divorced from the state of one's sexual fulfillment. The techniques I am discussing here are not like any other form of suggestion or metaphysics. I have recently been fortunate enough to discuss the results of these ideas with a small group of people who have already practiced them. They have found that the application of psycho-ecstasy techniques has changed their love life and with it has come a new realization of their own potentials on all levels. Far from creating additional burdens, the exercises and techniques discussed here have freed them for other pursuits by reducing the time and effort formerly given to the tensions and doubts inherent in unsatisfactory sex relations.

## PSE and Union of the Sexes

Here then are the "Ten Commandments" which must be followed if psycho-ecstasy is to be achieved during sexual union:

1. The proper time of year, month, day and hour is very important. Fred Adams, the eminent West Coast astrologer and philosopher, says, "The calendar is the backbone of knowledge." Living in tune with nature permits us to have greater access to the blessings of nature and thus realize ourselves to the fullest. This doesn't mean that you cannot have satisfactory sexual relations at any time regardless of the calendar, but if that rare and exalted state called psychic oneness that is part and parcel of psycho-ecstasy is desired, great care should be taken that the undertaking is planned for a propitious moment. Certainly the results of this venture will be different when undertaken during the "dark of the moon," with its disturbing, uncertain vibrations or just before the full moon with the rising tide of energy all around us in nature. It is wise to consult the moon tables and plan accordingly. This need not be done in a cold, calculating way at all, but by keeping oneself informed of the various phases of the moon, one is likely to have an inner feeling of the appropriate time. Of lesser impact are the movements of sun and planets, since the moon rules the emotional self within. Thus, the first commandment in this context must read, *"Be sure that time and tides are with you in your undertaking."*

2. The place where the encounter is to take place, the surroundings, the atmospheric conditions, and the general vibrations of locality are also very important. Ecstasy can never be achieved if the pressures of the environment are such that one is continually concerned with it to the point

where the power of unhappy thoughts intrudes and destroys a satisfactory building up of positive energies. Ideally the locality should be somewhere in the open, that is to say surrounded by open space. The more trees and greenery the better, and in an altitude that is neither too elevated nor too depressed. If the vibrations of close neighbors are permitted to influence the area of one's place, they will also interfere with the thought processes so necessary to reach the exalted state desired. The more empty space one can find to surround oneself with the better. I realize the difficulties and limitations of this command in our modern age, especially for city dwellers. An attempt should be made to be as private as possible when undertaking this quest. The greater amount of greenery surrounding the location will also contribute additional oxygen, a very necessary ingredient in the process. Next to the proper location, the sound level of the surrounding area is of considerable importance. Sound represents small particles of energy bombarding not only the human ear but the entire body, consequently great care must be taken to have a quiet place as well as an isolated one. It will do no good to find oneself on top of a mountain surrounded by forests if the echo of the highway just below intrudes continuously or if low flying airplanes overhead will disturb the peace of the setting every few minutes or so.

To a lesser degree, the light level is of importance. A bright sunlit place without mitigating shadows is not likely to produce harmonious vibrations; neither, for that matter, total darkness nor a heavily overcast sky. The ideal lies somewhere between these two extremes. A softly lit place shielded from the rays of the sun and yet reflecting the beneficial illumination of our life-giving star is probably the best if one has a chance to arrange this. If artificial light is used, great care should be taken that it is indirect, and under no circumstances should the so-called flourescent bulbs be used in such a room. They cast a very destructive form of light, and the radiation from these bulbs can actually be harmful. Contrary to what some people might expect, total darkness is neither desirable nor helpful. Many people prefer to make love in darkness. They do so not because darkness enhances the process but because within them, either consciously or unconsciously, is a sense of shame over what they are doing. Such a false evaluation of a natural process must never be permitted to exist. To the contrary, honest pride should be taken in one's physical appearance whether it is ideal or less than ideal, and subdued light conditions are best to permit visual contact between the partners. There is no need to "pull down the blinds," no need to "get under the cover," or to suggest in any way that one is about to do something that must be shielded from the prying eyes of the world. The setting itself is private enough. There should be nothing in the act itself that cannot be looked at simultaneously by the partners participating in it. It is important to accept one's appearance and one's actions as perfectly natural and to have pride in one's accomplishments in this connection.

The second commandment in this context therefore should stress, *"Select a proper location where you may have peaceful vibrations, a minimum of noise or other intrusions, and where you can truly relax in body, mind and spirit."*

3. Even in ordinary human relations the element of pressure is important. Anything hurried or obviously subject to time limitations is not likely to be very successful. The joy of achieving sexual union must never be trammeled by limitations of time. The very essence of full congress requires a

suspension of the time element within us, something not easily achieved even under ordinary conditions. But if outer limitations of business or social pressures are permitted to construct walls of time around the event one has in mind, then the result will surely be negative and disappointing from the very outset. Thus, a third commandment should remind the participants, *"It is necessary to suspend all notion of time and to create an atmosphere of unhurried, timeless pleasure when nothing matters but the desired objective."*

4. Finding the proper setting for the desired adventure and the elimination of intrusion is not enough. There is also the question of what I call the "magical element" to be considered. Flowers placed around the house or room will create a sense of beauty and peace. It is necessary to select flowers relating to the personality of the woman involved and stressing the colors she prefers. In addition to flowers, soft music played in the background has always been considered an inducement to love. Here it becomes part of a general build-up towards an even greater objective. The burning of incense will be helpful in clearing the atmosphere of impurities and of even further detaching one's thought from the mundane world outside. Clearly the placing of these elements takes time and good judgment. They must be in place prior to the arrival of the two partners, or at least of the woman. Under no circumstances should time be spent by the couple to do these things after they have reached the place where their union is to take place. The fourth commandment in the attempt to reach psycho-ecstasy in love must therefore consist of the reminder, *"Be sure and place flowers of the right kind into the room or house, play soft music in the background and burn incense to purify the air."*

## PSE and Union of the Sexes

5. If words are the keys to action then the proper spoken preamble will be of paramount importance to what may ensue. If the two participants arrive together, married or not, they should have certainly discussed their plans for the future while enroute. If they only meet at their destination a certain amount of time should be spent in light conversation touching on subjects of mutual interest or speaking of art, music or other subjects of an emotional nature. The conversation should steer away from anything controversial, political, or anything that is likely to draw in the world outside. Personal recollections, personal feelings, and impressions are good subjects, and if there is stiffness of attitude between the two lovers sometimes the ice can be broken through humor or the sharing of past experiences. Whenever verbalization is required, it should not deal with the love act itself. At this point the purpose of words is to relax the participants and to allow them to get to know each other better, even if they have known each other for many years on a mundane level. Whatever they say to each other now is of immediate importance to what is to follow. The more things they can find they have in common and talk about the better. It may be trifling things of importance only to themselves but it is important to bring these things out into the open. Gradually the conversation should steer towards a definition of what love means to them individually and as a couple. The fifth commandment therefore stresses, *"The verbalization of love and the contact between the participants on a word level is an important preamble to the acts that follow."*

6. It is important that one dresses properly for the occasion. Wearing ordinary clothes which one has worn the day before or many times are particularily out of place if they are

familiar to the opposite sex, and if they have been seen and worn before, they should not be worn on this occasion. The clothes selected need not be purchased fresh but they should come as a surprise to the partner. The element of surprise cannot be sufficiently stressed in this operation. Bright pleasant clothes, light clothes, a touch of the unusual, perhaps even a touch of the bizarre are entirely within keeping. Jewelry selected should be personal and individual and every effort should be made to create a unique impression through one's clothes and accessories. A general appearance of cleanliness and freshness is very important along with the clothes one wears. If the couple believes in short hair then by all means let the hair be short. If they are convinced that the natural way of growing one's hair long is preferable then let it be that way. But in either case, one dresses as if one is going on holiday or if one were to attend a special occasion of great importance which in fact one is. The sixth commandment refers to dress: *"Fresh clothes and accessories, preferably something one has not worn before, holiday finery or exceptional bright colors will enhance this initial appearance and work favorably, not only between the two partners, but for the person wearing them directly by giving him or her a sense of putting 'the best foot forward.' "*

7. Furtive light touching of hands or even faces during casual moving about is a good way of establishing physical contact. When speaking to each other, the two partners should embrace occasionally, lightly, in a natural way, or take each other's hands, or perhaps grab each other's arms when pointing out an object or the landscape in the distance through the windows. It is important to begin touching each other in a gradual, slow manner and not in a heavy, physi-

cally oriented way. The seventh commandment concerns itself with the proper "touch system." The delightful, electrifying experience of having one's sensory mirrors feel another person's skin must be allowed to develop slowly and gradually. *"Casual touch between the partners will build the necessary energies much more strongly than would an immediate, sudden thrust one for the other."*

8. Depending upon the previous relationship between the two participants, one of two avenues will now be taken. Sometimes a bath is indicated, symbolizing not only cleanliness both within and without, but also a desire to quickly get to the bare facts of life. Naturally, one undresses completely for a bath. If this is the road taken both partners should emerge wearing robes. Under no circumstance should they emerge naked. More likely, however, both partners will have taken baths prior to coming to the place of their intended adventure. Thus, the gradual undressing will be more important.

One of the reasons strip tease artists have been so successful in the entertainment world is the fact that the gradual, deliberate undressing by a woman is more likely to arouse the sexual instincts in the man than would sudden total nudity. Even without the knowledge and use of psycho-ecstatic techniques, the proper way to undress is of paramount importance in the love relationship both on the part of the woman and on the part of the man, though to a lesser degree.

One of the somewhat daring card games of the past few decades was a game called strip poker. Even though the final result was never in doubt, the build-up seemed to have created the necessary excitement and tension. Here we do not have any doubts about the outcome either. The reason why gradual undressing is important has nothing to do with the question of whether or not the sexual act will take place. The gradual undressing seems to heighten the sensual stimulation of both partners. As the body emerges in its natural state the two partners are able to slowly focus their attention upon their aims. There is also a certain advantage in the almost rhythmical, gradual disposal of clothing which can heighten the mutual interest between them. This can be even greater if one helps the other divest himself or herself of certain apparel. None of these details are particularly new, but it is important to remember them in this context since they are leading to the final stages where entirely new and involved techniques will be added to make the final results truly "out of this world." Commandment number eight should read, *"The proper way to undress is to do so slowly, deliberately, piecemeal, and to undress each other. With each falling piece of apparel a thought should go as the body emerges gradually in its natural state. That thought should visualize and mentally caress that part of the body which is now visible to the naked eye."*

9. The actual embrace comes next. This is not an attempt to describe in graphic details how men and women make love. I assume that anyone reading this book already knows this, but it is important that the lovemaking be gentle, gradual, and unhurried. The physical element dominates, although undoubtedly most couples will have feelings and thoughts of an endearing kind accompanying their actions at this stage. Full contact between the two anatomies is now taking place and within a matter of a few minutes or perhaps a half an hour the couple will be ready to reach the expected climax of their relationship. It is important that this climax

## PSE and Union of the Sexes

not be reached too quickly or too soon, and the skill of the individual will be tested in the sense that a degree of moderation is very necessary here if one is to achieve true psycho-ecstasy in the end. I do not for a moment say that this is easy to accomplish. In the excitement of passion few can measure their thoughts and actions to such a degree that they retain full control, but it must be attempted since the techniques of psycho-ecstasy cannot be injected into the process any earlier or any later than indicated. The ninth commandment in this context, therefore, must warn the lovers, *"Do not achieve climax too quickly and too much on the physical level, but maintain a steady arousal, caressing lovingly in both action and thought, and thinking continuous thoughts of further closeness, of greater union."*

10. Somewhere just before the final ascent to climax, the special techniques of psycho-ecstasy must be introduced by either one of the partners or preferably both. At this point the psychic power within is summoned quickly from the lower solar plexus as in previous situations and permitted to gather momentum as it rises upward to the upper solar plexus in the head. Tremendous energy will then be at the participants' disposal. The physical energies created by their congress will enhance the psychic energy within them, and if the proper moment has been chosen they will unite to create a formidable reservoir of strength. This should take no more than one or two minutes. When the power within the couple has reached the breaking point and they feel that they cannot hold on another moment it must be released one to the other as if they were sending forth electrical energies, providing each other with a radiation of an ecstatic nature. At that very moment the visualization of total union must take place.

## Psycho-Ecstasy

Both participants will then visualize themselves as no longer being separate entities but as two parts of a whole. This visualization of a total merger of personalities is perhaps the most important part of the psycho-ecstasy techniques. After holding the thought of total union between them for a few seconds, a few heart beats at the most, the physical interaction between them leading to climax, accompanied by a visualization and command to rise, rise, rise above themselves, will create a state of total ecstasy. It is impossible to describe that condition in words. Suffice it to say that it will last just a few seconds and yet will give the sensation of eternity to those experiencing it. There is nothing more to be done. They will maintain this state of bliss for as long as they can, gradually falling back upon the earth level as the power ebbs.

About the only unpleasant result of their union under these techniques is a state of total exhaustion immediately following it. For a few minutes they may be unable to speak or move. Gradually, the flow of energy returns and fills the void left by this total expansion of their psychic selves. Within a matter of half an hour or perhaps an hour, they will have regained a sense of equilibrium. They should rest for another hour or two, or perhaps for a night's sleep. At any rate, when they feel themselves sufficiently rested, they should rise, take a bath of salt water and slowly return to the world of ordinary human relationships. They must under no circumstances burst forth immediately, get dressed and run. They should, very gradually, step down their vibrations to ordinary levels. At first there should be light conversation followed by a walk in the garden or other such exercise. Then they should have a meal followed by a change of clothes

## PSE and Union of the Sexes

before they go their separate ways or return to their mundane occupations.

The tenth commandment in this set of instructions to reach psycho-ecstasy in sexual union must therefore be the most important of all: *"Just prior to reaching climax the two partners should arouse their inner psychic powers from the lower solar plexus and onto the upper solar plexus in their heads; then the visualization of total union of the two entities and the merging into one unit must be undertaken. After a few moments of this, they must visualize themselves rising above their ordinary level of consciousness to reach a state of total detachment and at the same time total bliss."*

There are certain auxiliary exercises which can be undertaken prior to the meeting of the two partners to enhance the final results. For several days prior to the intended adventure in love, it would be useful to visualize the coming together of the partners in whatever details one wishes to, but in a gradual, pleasant and dreamlike manner which does not dwell upon physical details so much as upon feelings. If one intermingles into these thoughts phrases of endearment that one expects to speak to the partner, they may very well create a friendly atmosphere upon actually meeting. It is important to remember that words are energy particles traveling from the mind of one person to the mind of another, and that they can implant themselves in another person and yield tangible results.

After PSE, psycho-ecstasy, has been accomplished on one occasion, one need not despair of repeating the process at some future date. It can never become a routine or a frequent undertaking, to be sure, but it may be repeated in various

*Psycho-Ecstasy*

ways, in various locations provided the same ten principles are observed and followed. It is best, however, that special locations be chosen in addition to the appropriate calendar facts, so that the highest state of emotional consciousness is not reached without some adequate reason or purpose. It is always best to have cause for a celebration when one reaches out into these exalted spheres. Celebrations after all mark certain happenings, are connected with emotional expressions, and are far more than merely a date in the calendar. If life cannot be one long celebration, then at least let it be punctuated and stressed by frequent celebration whenever there is reason by virtue of an important milestone in the life of one or the other participant.

Psychic powers drawn from within are used to create the highest state of emotional consciousness during sexual union just prior to climax. This power is derived from the energy particles within the personality, and it represents the life force with which all of us are born initially. The amount that can be raised differs widely in individuals, but the life force can be strengthened, no matter how much of it there is within us, through proper living, through proper breathing, and through proper thought processes.

Sexual union under these conditions creates the highest form of vibration known to man. Thus a psychic force a thousand times greater than the one expended to create the state of psycho-ecstasy will be returned to the individuals as a result of their union. It is wise to prepare for this strange cycle taking place immediately after the process and to direct these newly created energies back into the physical, mental, and spiritual apparatus known as personality. If properly done, the process of sexual union through psycho-ecstasy processes can actually perpetuate itself, creating new energies

## PSE and Union of the Sexes

in the process and increasing the supply within the individuals participating in the process. It is a long way from the animalistic, basic sexual instinct seeking only gratification for the moment, to the bliss of psycho-ecstasy created at the highest level of consciousness. But if man was created in God's image then he deserves that high state of exaltation and nothing less.

Perhaps a leaf should be taken from the pagan rituals of lovemaking here, since they come closest to expressing the true sentiments of a couple totally in tune with nature. Where I have referred to verbalizations of sentiment during the actual lovemaking and just prior to the application of psycho-ecstasy techniques and the raising of the power within, I had in mind phrases similar in intent, if not actual construction, to the following: Both partners mentally divide up the body and the personality of the opposite member into various parts or sections. They will start from the feet and work their way up to the head. There is no hard and fast rule as to the actual words chosen for the expression of endearment. Whatever the imagination of the individual permits may be used. For instance, one might say, "I touch your delicate feet, my love,————." Ultimately touch, kiss, admire and caress using these terms to create a greater sense of variety. The focal points should be the feet, legs, knees, sexual organ, back, chest or breasts, neck, shoulder, face, lips, eyes and the crown of the head. Take turns in expressing your admiration for one particular zone of the body of the partner. "I caress the perfectly formed legs of my beloved" may be followed by, "I touch the knees of my love in endearment," or some similar expression. This is not only a poetic way of saying what is in one's heart, but it also creates additional stimulation and excitement. The touch must actually be applied, of course, and the kiss and the caressing must also take place as these words are spoken. However, they should be applied lightly, not in the height of passion. When all zones of the body have been lovingly mentioned by both partners and the head reached, they should clasp hands, embrace and exclaim together, "Now we shall engulf ourselves in the mainstream of love for a more perfect union," or some such expression of intended oneness. These verbalizations are very important. The love act itself is meaningless without the proper thought behind each and every step. As a matter of fact, the mechanical action is nothing but a carrying out of the emotional, mental intent. Without the meaning of each and every move, no stimulation of any depth can be accomplished. Ultimately the act of lovemaking is a symbolic expression of inner longing to unite with another human being. It is not a purpose unto itself, nor can it be performed to any degree of ecstatic fulfillment without proper graduation, proper preparation and, at all times, a full understanding of the inner meanings of each and every step. Depending upon the vocabularies of the two partners, phrases will be made up to suit the occasion. The more poetic these phrases are, while at the same time being explicit and understandable, the better for the results. They should spring from spontaneous excitement rather than from a slow, logical process however, and should not be prepared beforehand. Comparing various zones of the body to forces of nature, to portions of the bodies of the gods or any such exalted comparison is a good way of creating a higher consciousness in oneself and preparing the road towards the ultimate consummation in total psycho-ecstasy.

If this adventure into lovemaking is done with all due preparations and following explicitly the PSE techniques I have described in this chapter, then the memory of the occasion will be with you forever. Subsequent occasions of this kind will be different yet parallel the first one, and each occasion will become unique, while at the same time creating a feeling of a renewal, a wedding and mating of two souls and bodies each time. It will leave the participants with the sensation of having experienced eternal spring, time and again.

*Chapter XIII*

# The Drugless Trip: How to Get High through Psycho-Ecstasy

Earlier in this book I had discussed the inadvisability of using drugs to create a state of detachment from reality, supposedly to enter certain regions of consciousness that promise to be at once exciting and pleasurable to the one undertaking the venture. The medical reasons need not therefore be discussed here again. Even if there were not any medical reasons, I would still be against the injection of foreign substances into the bloodstream of the body. Lately medical authorities have altered their view even concerning marijuana—"grass," as it is commonly called. Constant usage of this mild hallucinogenic can also alter the physical system and is therefore dangerous to health.

Nevertheless, the desire to lift oneself out of the ordinary, to experience a multilevel, multidimensional exaltation, persists and is by no means an unhealthy sign. Man has a right to demand a "trip" into regions not hitherto explored. The desire does not necessarily indicate a dissatisfaction or inability to cope with the present surroundings or the world in which one functions. Frequently this is, of course, the case, and the trip becomes an escape hatch from reality. But in a sufficient number of cases I am familiar with, the idea of taking a trip into the regions of mind expansion is not motivated by any desire to use this as a crutch in ordinary life. To the contrary, these are people with well-balanced professional lives, emotionally stable but somehow in need of additional, wider horizons in their mental expansion. To them the trip represents an adventure into the unknown and is comparable to an exciting journey to a foreign land one has never before visited. They hope to bring back valuable memories which, in turn, will help them make their ordinary lives more colorful and meaningful. In condemning the use of hallucinatory drugs, I am therefore not hitting primarily at the hippies, the dropouts, the misguided element among the young. I am hitting equally at adults who lead well-adjusted lives and attempt to add to these lives through artificial stimulation.

The term "trip" is not as farfetched as one might surmise. Some travel actually does take place. When there is disassociation of personality, the bonds between the conscious and unconscious are loosened. All those who have had psychic experiences are familiar with a state called astral projection or out-of-the-body experiences. In this condition the inner self, the seat of personality, is ejected voluntarily or deliberately, either during sleep or while fully awake, into the

## The Drugless Trip

dimension generally called the world of the mind or the ether. In this rarified dimension, all spiritual life continues and the ejected individual may very well meet up with those who have gone on before him or he'll meet up with others who are still in the flesh but have also managed to travel astrally. The classic work dealing with astral projection *(Phenomena of Astral Projection)* is by Sylvan Muldoon and Dr. Hereward Carrington. Thousands of people have experienced the sensation of being ejected from their bodies and finding themselves flying rapidly over an unknown landscape or coming down in front of people they know well. Occasionally, they are even observed in their spiritual form and bring back valuable data which they later check out and find to be correct. These cross-correspondences have established beyond a doubt that astral projection is a reality, that people can indeed leave their physical bodies behind temporarily and travel great distances in a fraction of a second. Some time does lapse, but the amount of time elapsed is so small that the trip seems simultaneous with the ejection of the personality from the physical body. The majority of these experiences take place during sleep. The telltale mark of true astral projection, as against the ordinary dream, is the sensation of falling from great heights rapidly in a spin or other circular movements, and to wake up finding oneself in bed sometimes drenched with sweat, sometimes exhausted as if one had walked for miles. The sensation of falling from great heights is an illusion, however. It represents the physical reaction to the "stepping down" of the vibrations of the personality or the etheric body. When a person returns from travelling in the ether, the speed of the body movement must be reduced to accommodate the lower speed of the physical body. This is accomplished fairly quickly at the point of return and creates the sensation of falling, when in effect it is nothing more than breaking a fall.

Astral projection also takes place while fully awake. There are a number of cases on record where a person would rest quietly and suddenly find himself standing next to his physical body looking down at it as if it were another person, or a person might have the sensation of giddiness and find himself floating up from his physical duplicate. The floating would continue until the ceiling is reached at which point the trip stops. This is so because the traveller knows very well that he cannot go through the ceiling. However, he *can* if he realizes that his physical body is not involved. If he projects himself further willfully, he will, of course, go right through the ceiling and out into the landscape. If he accepts the ceiling of his room as the limitation of his travel, he will slowly drift down until he reaches his physical body and then quickly snap into place. This snapping into place has been observed by many people, and it is instantaneous and occasionally uncomfortable. There is never any danger involved, nor is astral projection in the slightest comparable to mental derangement or the psychotic state. During surgery, when certain drugs have been administered, people will occasionally experience ejection of this kind and find themselves hovering above their physical bodies, observing, as it were, how their bodies are being treated by the surgeons.

Controlled experiments in astral projection have also been undertaken. Some years ago I was present when a psychic gentleman was directed to astrally project himself to an apartment some twenty blocks distant. At the other end of the experiment, a group had prepared a room with certain telltale marks. A flower had been placed into a vase, a book had been opened at a certain page, and other simple and

## The Drugless Trip

easily observed objects placed in the way. The young man returned several minutes later from his astral trip and accurately reported what he had seen at the other end. Since none of the group with him knew of the arrangements in the other apartment, he could not have gotten this information from the unconscious of those around him. The experiment therefore was a complete success.

But astral projection is primarily a trip into locations other than where one is at the time, and occasionally a trip to explore other dimensions where one might meet up with people who have gone on before. It is not truly an exploration of one's own potential, nor does it expand consciousness in any way, beyond a greater sense of exhilaration which comes with being freed of the shackles of the physical body. What we want to retain from this sensation, however, is the marvelous feeling of limitless movement, of weightlessness, and of the ability to travel at great speed. The sensation has always played a part in the excitement of the senses. It can be used to great advantage when dealing with psychic expansion. What is needed, however, is a different direction than the direction to the *outside* implied in astral projection of the inner self.

Here is how you accomplish the "drugless" trip into the realm of PSE, psycho-ecstasy:

1. Make yourself as comfortable as you can wearing as little clothing as you wish or as you are comfortable with. Be sure you are undisturbed unless, of course, you wish to take the trip together with another person. In that case, make sure there are no conflicts between you, and that you are in full accord as to what you are about to do. The place must be quiet, not too warm and not too brightly lit. A couch or

comfortable chair is best, and some air should enter to avoid the stuffiness that sometimes may be detrimental to your health while in the expanded consciousness state.

2. Define as sharply as you can the purpose of your trip. Do you wish to experience exaltation of the senses in general, or is it a specific purpose you have in mind? That is to say, do you wish to hear musical sounds other than those you are accustomed to? Do you wish to experience a color sensation, or do you wish to experience some other specific stimulation connected with one or more of your five senses? Generally speaking, people attempting this method of getting out of themselves should be doing so with the broadest possible point of view. That is to say, simply desire to experience ecstasy on all its levels and in as many forms as it may take, involving as many of your senses as possible. Later, when you have mastered this technique you may add specific limitations in order to enhance one particular area of the sensations.

3. Breathe deeply about a dozen times, expanding your chest while you do it. Anyone familiar with yoga techniques will already realize that this heightens your state of consciousness.

4. Next, stretch your body several times slowly and maintain the position of complete extension of the muscles for a few seconds at a time. This will relax your physical apparatus to the point where body resistance to the techniques to be applied will be minimal or nonexistent.

5. Rub your palms together rapidly and with great force for about a minute, then hold the palms close to your

## The Drugless Trip

forehead at a distance of about a quarter of an inch. This will create a sensation of heat and vibrations. You have raised electromagnetic energy in this manner and are now feeding this body energy back into your solar plexus.

6. Close your eyes, lean back and visualize yourself being in a dark room, except for one light source in the ceiling. You hold the thought of being in this dark room in a comfortable position staring at the imaginary light source above you. You do this for about a minute, concentrating in a relaxed but firm way on the light source within your mind. This will draw you away from whatever influences still intrude from the outside world.

7. With your eyes firmly closed, with your lips closed, and in a very relaxed physical condition, you now begin to suggest to yourself that you rise from the ground. The sensation of becoming lighter and lighter will follow. Do not be alarmed by a certain giddiness. This is an illusion and you are not actually getting dizzy. Maintain this suggestion to yourself for about a minute. You will find yourself slowly arising within yourself, so to speak. Suggest next that you are reaching the level of the light in the dark room of your imagination. Hold this position indefinitely, that is until you are giving yourself another order. Now as you float at the level of the bright light in the dark room of your imagination, you reach down into the depth of your personality and command your psychic forces to assemble, visualizing them as shapeless and invisible, yet tangible and powerful at the same time. Order the psychic forces to rise and enter your upper solar plexus at the top of your head. You will experience a certain sense of heaviness in your head at this time. Even if you have the desire to topple over, mentally that is,

## Psycho-Ecstasy

do not give in to it. When you have the conviction that all of your psychic force has risen into the upper solar plexus at the top of your head, release the command of floating at the level of the imaginary light and prepare yourself for the next step.

8. Command your astral body to go on an inner trip, that is to say, expand consciousness within but not to leave the physical body at any time. Do this by visualizing the astral being forced deeper into your physical body as if it were bursting at the seams. The strain will become quite apparent as you do this. Do not be alarmed by this feeling. Within a few seconds the strain will disappear and you will experience a feeling of great freedom as if you were floating. With your eyes still firmly closed you will then start to experience great expansions of color, sound and other elements relating to your five senses.

9. Observe these simulations for about a minute or two. Do not open your eyes but release the pressure of your lips. Start humming a sound similar to *om*. Start lowly and in a low voice, increasing the sound and level as you go along. When you reach the highest pitch, hold the high pitch for about thirty seconds then slowly go back until the hum becomes inaudible and disappears altogether. Repeat this three times. It will add to the power which you have raised from within yourself.

10. With your eyes still closed breathe rapidly a dozen times. If a dozen seems too much and you find yourself actually becoming dizzy, start first with four or five rapid breathing exercises. Ultimately, a dozen will not harm you.

## The Drugless Trip

At this point you should be fully on your way to whatever this trip will bring you. Lie still with your eyes closed as if you were sleeping. The experience will last from five to fifteen minutes and when you feel yourself "coming down" again do not open your eyes immediately. Instead, wait until you hear your pulse beat and become conscious of your surroundings again.

At this point you may open your eyes, breathe slowly a few times and stretch. Get up very gradually and eventually return to your normal pursuits. It is important to drink a glass of water immediately afterwards, as the psychic energy expended will have depleted your reservoir of moisture. Do not eat any solid food for at least a half hour after the experience. If you have undertaken this trip during the daytime you will find yourself very tired come nightfall. Do not be alarmed by this, it is a natural reaction. It is unwise to undertake this experiment more than once or twice a week. Psychic energies raised and expended to deplete the vital force within. Carefully marshalled however, these forces will be self-renewing and the experience will greatly enrich your storehouse of emotional stimuli. There will be no weird monsters or fantasy creatures populating your dreams, nor will there be anything frightening in this kind of trip. What you experience is largely mind expansion into positive realms, areas which your ordinary five senses cannot touch normally, but which they are capable of reaching provided they are given a boost.

Two or more people may undertake this trip together, of course, with varying results. I would not recommend anyone attempting group trips unless and until they have also succeeded by themselves first. Ideally, a male and female undertaking the trip together would experience parallel sensations.

## Psycho-Ecstasy

There might be a light touching of hands but other than that no physical contact. An additional advantage of a dual trip is the possibility that the psychic reservoir of one person is larger than that of the other, thus creating a pool of energies shared equally by both people.

It is of course understood that the consciousness expanding trip of this kind towards the realm of psycho-ecstasy must never be undertaken if the person attempting it has also been taking any kind of drug beforehand. By drug I do not only mean the conventional psychedelic substances, or even the unconventional hallucinogenics such as certain mushrooms or plants, but even alcohol, strong coffee, large amounts of cola or substantial amounts of nicotine. The cleaner the blood stream is prior to embarking upon this particular trip, the greater the results. Personality expansion through PSE, psycho-ecstasy, does not require additional stimulation by artificial means. It is an end unto itself.

## Chapter XIV

# Bridging the Gulf

Lack of communication between certain groups seems to be one of the chief reasons why our world is in the disoriented state it seems to be in. When two entities, whether they are people or ideas, fail to communicate with each other and establish a link, they become self-sufficient and eventually isolated from each other. The continuing exchange of data between these entities is of paramount importance if there is to be any progress. In ancient times, and especially during the Middle Ages, lack of communication was physical. That is to say, one part of the world knew nothing about the other part simply because no one had gone there and come back and reported about it. This had to do with the primitive state of travel and physical transportation, of course. In modern

## Psycho-Ecstasy

times we do not have to travel great distances to be informed about strange lands or different people. Since the inventions of technology have brought distant aspects of our planet within everyone's reach, ignorance about different countries and different people is no longer a matter of opportunity, but of desire or omission, as the case may be. On the national level the lack of communication can be disastrous. Lack of understanding leads to war and to failure to learn from war when it does occur.

When there is no adequate communication between two poles then we speak of an existing gulf. This gulf is simply the absence of contact. There is first of all a gulf between the sexes. Men taken as a group do not see their status the same as women see it. Conversely, women would like to alter their own status from another point of view than the prevailing male attitude towards them. Out of frustrations are born such movements as Women's Liberation Movement. The gulf between the sexes exists on several levels. First of all, on the purely animalistic, physical level. The fact that man procreates and that woman is dependent on his willful action prior to conceiving has always given man a feeling of dominance. In our society this has led to a careless and utter disregard of woman's needs and responsibilities and to a sexual promiscuity that masks a sense of irresponsibility with a professed intent to "liberate" and equalize the woman. If woman is to be free and equal, then surely man does not have to care whether or not his action renders a woman pregnant. Surely such a woman should be proud to rear her child without help from the other partner. Unfortunately, society on the whole has not seen fit to accept this attitude, and the gulf between the sexes is largely due to the conflict between a liberated attitude on the part of many women and a total inability of our society to accept this on any large scale. What results is a sense of resentment. Polarization by sexes inevitably follows, which in turn will not be conducive to the development of the love instinct and a gentle approach to companionship which is so necessary to create the higher state of consciousness between the sexes. Secondly, the tension between male and female is also due to a clear-cut advantage man possesses over woman in the matter of employment and professional standing. Despite liberalization, despite an enlightened attitude on the part of a few individuals, there is still an entire body of pursuits and professions not open to women at all, or if it is open to a female candidate then that candidate is subjected to far more rigorous tests than her male competitor would be.

When a woman is accepted into a predominantly male profession or business, and even if she manages to maintain her position by sheer extra effort, she will remain an island isolated by her surroundings and by no means accepted on equal terms. The very fact that woman is "soft" and bears children is being held against her in many areas of professional activities. She is discriminated against in salaries, in rights, and in the matter of advancement. This is not merely a tendency among the Western or capitalistic societies, it is prevalent even under communism. Except for the period of pregnancy, when anatomical differences clearly indicate the need for a different approach to a woman seeking employment than to a man desiring the same position, woman is capable of performing in exactly the same manner as her male counterpart would be. The gulf between sexes, however, is based largely on tradition and on an inherited tendency to look upon womanhood as a reserved, limited part of humanity.

## Psycho-Ecstasy

Partially responsible for this condescending attitude are some religious denominations as well. The Christian church holds a dim view of women entering the public life to any degree. Christianity prefers womanhood to be centered in the home, or if a woman is to be actively engaged in public work then it should be in a charitable or health service, which are essentially female-oriented to begin with. For different reasons, Eastern religions also relegate women to subordinate positions. There are very few religions in which a woman may attain priesthood. The "old religion," also called Wicca, and a few enlightened protestant denominations are about the only ones which come to mind. In Eastern religions woman is permitted in the sacred precincts of the temple, not as a dominant intellectual factor but as a visual adornment such as the Japanese temple dancers or the soothsayer in primitive religions where fortune telling is still part of the religious practice. In addition, of course, a woman candidate has always had an uphill fight, since many of her constituents are male and resent either openly or unconsciously being represented by a woman. To surmount such strikes against one merely because one is of the female gender requires special fortitude and perhaps special techniques such as the application of psycho-ecstasy.

The gulf between age groups is just as difficult to bridge as the one between the sexes. It consists of a different kind of view on almost everything ranging from politics to economics, to personal hygiene, to clothes, even to the spoken language. The young resent the old because they feel that the old are running things; the old resent the young because they *are* young and because they are rebellious in spirit. The ones in the middle, those neither too young nor too old, resent both extremes. They resent the young because they no longer are quite as young as they would like to be to satisfy their appetites in various areas, and they resent the old because they feel the old are not relinquishing their positions fast enough to suit them. Economically, there is discrimination against the young in some areas of employment. The very young do not get full salaries until they reach the age where they presumably can start families. This does not take into account individual ability or effort, it is merely and arbitrarily decided that a certain age limit must be reached before a man can earn a full salary. There is, of course, far more discrimination against the old, who are thought to be unemployable in some quarters. An older man starting off on a job may have to take less than someone somewhat younger would have demanded. After fifty, especially in America, a man is on his way downhill in the eyes of the business community and therefore should be satisfied with a modest remuneration. Comparatively best-off is the large middle group in their middle twenties, thirties and early forties. They are thought to be in the prime of their activities and therefore can demand top remunerations. Evaluating people by age groups is always unfair and dangerous since it overlooks the individual contribution a person can make regardless of age. There are no hard and fast rules on when a man develops talent or ability to perform a certain task. Age, in fact, is one of the most misleading characteristics when it comes to accomplishment.

In the arena of personal mores, of morality, and the attitude towards society and religion, the gulf between the ages is even more pronounced. By and large the young take it upon themselves to demand great freedom in making their own moves and their own evaluations as to what is right and what is wrong. Older people, on the other hand, tend to be conservative for no other reason than to cling to that which they have been brought up with or have found to be effective in their struggle for success and recognition. In this the young tend to be more honest than the old. The young express themselves more freely and more basically regardless of the consequences, while the old will cover up any basic intentions even if they are feeling that they are right.

Young people are daring, old people cautious. That is why teenagers and men in their early twenties make such good soldiers. They go into battle unaware of the high stakes involved, somehow hoping they will survive. Older men would be far more hesitant in performing their duties as soldiers. Every army knows that a man after twenty-five makes poor soldier material. He cares too much about his skin. But not only in war do young people take chances. Motorcycle riding, auto racing, circus acrobatics, any profession or hobby calling for great daring and skill, even chance taking, will find its followers primarily among the very young. The older a man gets the more factors he will evaluate before making a decision. Young people tend to act more impulsively, and more emotionally for that matter. This doesn't necessarily mean that they are always wrong and that the aged person is always right. Frequently the impulse decision of the young gets closer to the truth than the cautious, logical deliberation of the older person. Again individuals alone count. Although some older people love to be part of the younger generation by dressing the part, by associating with them, and by honestly thinking and feeling as young people generally do, it requires more than good intentions to truthfully belong to the younger generation if one is not naturally born into it. That missing factor is an emotional one. If one can feel, react, identify, and above all

## Bridging the Gulf

communicate as the young do, then one has truly mastered the most difficult task of them all, to transcend the age gap and turn the clock back.

Bridging the age gap is just as important as bridging any other gap between groups because a gap tends to lead to polarization, to violence, to hostility, and ultimately to total isolation. Gaps between age groups may be the forerunners of social upheavals. If nothing else, they certainly destroy any form of warmth between members of varying age groups, any kind of interaction of mutual concern. To overcome this gap it is necessary to employ above all a great deal of good will, prejudice-free understanding, and learning. Sometimes even that is not enough. It is here that individuals may overcome the difficulties of the existing age gap by the application of psycho-ecstasy techniques and by thus individually accomplishing something that their group as a whole cannot do as a group. The result, of course, is just as beneficial if enough individuals follow this road.

Gulfs in the economic groups have in the past represented major problems in the development of trust among human beings. They do not do this to such a great degree today, as the boundaries between the rich and poor tend to be less absolute. The poor are getting richer and the rich are getting poorer. Developing in between them is a large middle class with substantial gains and less concern for economic security than their forefathers had in the late nineteenth century. Nevertheless, the gulf between extremes of economic stature still exists and creates problems. Economic gulfs can best be overcome through educational accomplishments and by the display of emotional concern between parties of different backgrounds. The coming society will undoubtedly evaluate cultural accomplishments at least as highly as economic achievements and thus even out any imbalance between groups as time goes on.

Somewhat similar is the situation concerning cultural inequities. The gulf between the uneducated and the well-educated has narrowed down considerably due to the great availability of educational facilities. In the process, the educational standards have also been lowered. But the broad mass of people everywhere can nowadays partake of a reasonably complete strata of education.

Since so much educational accomplishment deals with human well-being, health, welfare, development of natural resources and other essentials, this process of broadening of education must be counted on the plus side regardless of the fact that it has brought down the *standards* of information of education in general.

Since the gulf exists not only between groups as a whole but also individuals within those groups, they are best attacked on an individual level. PSE, psycho-ecstasy techniques, can indirectly contribute to a smoothing-out of these gulfs. Here is how it works. Any individual wishing to overcome a particular gulf existing between himself and another individual in whatever area under discussion will, first of all, discover within himself the area or areas of his strongest talent, some particular interest that is stronger within himself than other interests. It is important to discover and isolate that particular bent. Having discovered what one's strong points are, one then determines to increase one's potential in those areas and leave other areas out for the moment. For example, if a particular person's talent is music, he or she will invoke the psychic power within for the purpose of increasing this talent and of strengthening the ability to communicate this musical talent to other people. The power is

## Bridging the Gulf

raised in the manner already described in an earlier chapter. Once the power has risen to the upper solar plexus in the head, it is sent out in the direction of the other individual one wishes to reach. At the same time clothe it with the connotation of one's particular talent. The rising power creates an increased state of self-confidence. This can be developed to the point where the conviction ensues that one's special talent is outstanding to the point of being unique. One comes to regard oneself as an extraordinary human being whose negative qualities in other areas are merely the ways of nature, and compensating factors. From this feeling comes a sense of importance and mounting inner excitement. One is a chosen person able to do things others cannot do in quite the same way. The more one contemplates this state of things, and meditates on one's particular talent, the more one lifts oneself up into the higher realms of psychic consciousness culminating in a sense of joyfulness, bordering on, if not in fact entering, the realms of psycho-ecstasy. One has done this by one's own powers, first raising the inner psychic powers and then sending them out specifically programmed, as it were, to perform a limited and narrowly defined task.

The gulf between the sexes, between age groups, between economic and educational groups is being bridged by the efforts of the *individual* attempting it. One's outstanding, shining qualities are so strong that they overcome the limiting factors caused by the gulf between oneself and the other person.

For instance: A young person might fall in love with an older person, even though they are clearly of different generations, different economic and cultural backgrounds, and not truly suited for each other in the ordinary sense of the term. Nevertheless, the older partner is a great poet and his poetry has such power that it sways the younger person to forget all about the older person's shortcomings. Or an older person becomes deeply attracted to a much younger partner even though the younger person lacks education, breeding, and knowledge in many areas, but the young person has a unique tone of voice, a quality that is extraordinarily beautiful. That alone is sufficient to overcome obvious limitations and allow such a partnership to be harmonious and lasting. This does not merely apply in the areas of art or emotions. It applies equally in mundane situations. Physical unattractiveness, health hazards, poor background, any limiting factor can at times be totally overlooked, even outweighed, by other elements in that person's makeup, when these elements are so strong that they outweigh parallel elements in the ordinary human being. This is not a matter of logical choice or cool evaluation on the part of the one making the decision. It is an emotional impulse-motivated move which is instantaneous and usually very strong. To overcome the gulf let the one who wishes to overcome it shine somewhere or in something. He will then no longer be a member of a particular group, but an individual totally disconnected from the group characteristics, whatever they may be.

Psycho-ecstasy can be a great help in bridging the gap between these groups. The application of these techniques results neither in a condescending attitude nor in a need for adulation. The two individuals relate to each other on completely equal terms but bring into the relationship different points of view, different backgrounds, and often contradictory situations. These differences are nevertheless reconciled in the long run by the total process of interrelationship. Not too many individuals have outstanding qualities to stress under ordinary circumstances, even though these may be within them *latently*. Those who have such qualities and are unable to exteriorize them, or those who have incipient extraordinary qualities and abilities and wish to increase them, can do so through the application of PSE, psycho-ecstasy techniques. There need not be any further fear that the gulf between vastly different groups of people must also become the dividing line between them, and that individuals cannot overcome seeming limitations at will. They can and they should, so that ultimately we become one human race regardless of age, nationality, background or outer characteristics.

The sole remaining differential must then be the state of development of the human soul and that is as it should be: Ecstasy within, development without. While the techniques of psycho-ecstasy described in this work seem deceptively simple, they are quite complicated when one takes into account that so many imponderable factors must be considered at the same time while applying the techniques. If one or the other element is disregarded, the techniques simply won't work. Emotional factors have validity only to the person experiencing them. What is sent forth from that person and is at that moment still part of his inner emotional process will, however, influence another person into starting an emotional process of his or her own. In the interreaction of the two emotional processes lies the third element of gain and development, and it is this third factor that makes psycho-ecstasy, the reaching out into the higher realms of consciousness, possible.

Among some pagan groups, the idea of a personal god, in the sense Western religions have depicted him, or a god derived from the worship of a great master of the past as the East sees it, does not exist. Instead these pagan groups postulate "you are god," meaning that we are all part of the godhead and that there is nothing out there beyond that which we cannot comprehend. If the deity is the sum total of the devine spark within all of us strung together loosely through interrelationship and communication of various kinds, then the deity is clearly composed of positive and negative factors. If that be so, then the positive or good alone cannot create the godhead but must, of necessity, rely upon the existence of the negative or evil factor for the purpose of manifesting in full.

But when the pagan says, "you are god," he really does not mean this in the literal sense. What is implied is instead the idea that you are a mature human being and that your decisions must be your guiding influence. As you decide so you will be. As you are so you will feel. As you feel so you will progress. As you progress so you will learn. As you learn so you will reach the highest realms of consciousness. When you have reached those higher realms you will go on to other incarnations, or if you have already reached the exalted state where a return is no longer mandatory, you will merge eventually back into the godhead and thus rekindle the eternal energy pattern called life.

"You are god" also signifies that you are guiltless and need not fret over the concept of fear. Whatever you do is the result of your decision and you must live by it. The consequences will appear soon enough. There is nothing in nature that says you must always make good decisions. There is, in fact, no such thing as good and evil as absolutes. Both positive and negative factors are necessary to create energy, just as in the electrical process the tension between the unequal poles is absolutely necessary to create the flow of particles. Psycho-ecstasy techniques should be applied only

## Bridging the Gulf

when you, in your considered judgment, feel that there is need for it. You are your own decision maker and need not pay homage to any superior power other than that part of the natural law which operates in and through you. You are free, as free as you dare be. You are also responsible not only to yourself and to those with whom you have interrelations, but also to the natural law which has put you into this state of consciousness.

The potential to reach the exalted spheres of psycho-ecstatic consciousness is within each and every one of us. It is as much a birthright as the breathing of the air around us, but as the state of psycho-ecstasy once reached will inevitably reflect our inner selves, it is vitally important to be in tune with the universe and at peace with one's self. Only when the self, in its limited, earthly, narrow connotation has sufficiently overcome that state, can PSE, psycho-ecstasy, result in true bliss and fulfillment.